Powers and Duties *of a* Governor

PRINCIPLES, LAWS, AND LESSONS FROM MAINE

Powers and Duties *of a* Governor

PRINCIPLES, LAWS, AND LESSONS FROM MAINE

Derek P. Langhauser

Great Life Press
Second Edition, 2024

Second Edition ISBN: 978-1-938394-86-7
Library of Congress Control Number: 2022921049

Published by
Great Life Press
Rye, New Hampshire
www.greatlifepress.com

Front cover photo: Acadia National Park, by Courtney Rog.
Back cover photo: The author's faithful companion visiting the Governor's office, by the author.

Contents

Summary of Contents

To Annie, may she find through her own career in the law opportunity, challenge and reward.

"A constitutional democracy like ours is perhaps the most difficult of man's social arrangements to manage successfully. Our scheme of society is more dependent than any other form of government on knowledge and wisdom and self-discipline for the achievement of its aims. For our democracy implies the reign of reason on the most extensive scale."

Youngstown Sheet & Tube Co. v. Sawyer, 343 U.S. 579, 593 (1952) (Frankfurter, J., concurring)

"The difficulty with [the] conventional wisdom about the political limits of constitutional law is that it undervalues the place of constitutional discourse and decision in political dialogue. By debating our deepest differences in the shared language of constitutional rights and responsibilities, we create the possibility of persuasion and even moral education in our national life."

L. Tribe, American Constitutional Law, 13 (1st ed. 1978), citing A. Cox, The Role of the Supreme Court in American Government, 117 (1976)

Preface to Second Edition

This book was first published in 2022. This second edition contains additional edits and adds substantive analysis on two subjects. The first discusses the factors typically considered in deciding to permit a bill to become law without signature rather than signing or vetoing it. The second is a new chapter developing more fully the legal roots and conceptual elements underlying the power and duty of faithful execution. I hope that this book continues to serve as a valuable orientation and guide to Governors and their counsel.

DPL
Portland, Maine
February, 2024

Preface

This book is a compendium of the laws that govern and inform the powers and duties of a Governor. It identifies best practices, includes maxims of lessons learned, and is organized to allow for quick reference. Based primarily on Maine law, this book may educate and orient new Governors, counsel and staff—who are often new to the unique responsibilities of their position—on the conceptual character and practical scope of gubernatorial powers and duties, and the daily tasks of governing.

This book derives from my experience as a chief legal counsel for two Maine Governors, one a Republican and one a Democrat, who served 25 years apart. It is also informed by my work as a non-partisan counsel to several Maine Attorneys General and a state Senate President, constitutional counsel to a United States Senator, and law clerk to two state Supreme Court justices. The diverse roles and viewpoints of these officers have informed my perspective on those gubernatorial powers and duties that endure and prevail despite the partisanship or issues of the day.

Speed is often required in a Governor's office, so this book is organized and formatted to provide quick reference to the core sources. This edition is based on those laws and opinions reported as of June, 2022. In Maine, the principal sources for the Governor's powers and duties are found:

- Throughout the Maine Constitution, particularly Articles III (various lawmaking), V (all executive), and IX (various, including oaths, commissions, and tenure of officers).

- Throughout the Maine Revised Statutes, particularly Titles 1 (freedom of access), 2 (authority and some duties), 3 (nominations), 5 (finance and personnel), 15 (pardons), 21-A (elections), and 37-B (emergency management).

- In Opinions of the Justices that technically are advisory but are often precedential. These are sometimes, but not always, cited in the Maine Revised Statutes Annotated Notes of Decisions and they are regularly cited in Attorney General Opinions. Reported judicial opinions from fully litigated cases are few in number for a variety of reasons, such as intra-governmental issues, case/controversy.

- In Attorney General Opinions that technically are also advisory but are often helpful. A complete set of these Opinions can be found at *https://www.maine.gov/legis/lawlib/lldl/agops/agmaster.html.* They may be best searched by section of law using the search feature of an internet browser (as opposed to a search feature of the webpage itself).

- In *Tinkle, The Maine State Constitution (2nd ed. 2013)*, which recounts the history of constitutional provisions and cites leading opinions by both the Justices and the Attorney General.

In addition to these sources, this book cites many lesser-known or harder-to-find sources. These include U.S. Attorney General opinions, analogous federal sources, select scholarly articles, an ALI Restatement, rules of parliamentary procedure, a federal district court hearing transcript, agency regulations, state Superior Court opinions, and select Federalist Papers. In all instances, I have attempted to cite sources in a form that has prioritized ease of reading over strict style manual compliance.

I have benefited immeasurably from the excellent research by Nancy Rabasca and careful editing by Amy Homans, Helen Pelletier, Emma Akrawi, and Holly Peterson. Numerous other colleagues also contributed suggestions that I have valued and I very much appreciate all who helped.

This book is a culmination of much of my career; a career made possible by those who provided me with extraordinary opportunities: the clients who have trusted me and the judges who have mentored me. They have been role models and friends alike. I hope that they find this book worthy of their standards.

DPL
Portland, Maine
December, 2022

I.
Advising and Representing a Governor: Guiding Maxims

The lengthy text that follows this chapter identifies, organizes and details the many provisions of law that govern and inform the Governor's powers and duties. Governor's legal counsel and staff will of course first be drawn to the text of these sources in assessing an issue. But speed will require that the task quickly turn to translating, informing and advising the Governor about how the pertinent laws may be faithfully executed.

It is that task—of being effective with and for the Governor—that is the essential challenge of the job. To be done well, the role requires insights beyond mere legal analysis. It requires sound contextual judgment.

Accordingly, this work starts with a set of insights, based on my own diverse experiences, that I have reduced to the following maxims. Counsel and staff may find it helpful to keep these in mind as they move into the details of the sections that follow.

A. Work Ways of the Counsel

1. Power politics is full of sycophants and zealots. Your job is to never be either.

2. Have the courage to tell truth to power, especially on issues of consequence.

3. All your actions and conversations with others reflect on the character and values of the Governor. In those conversations, ask questions, gather information, express interest, but limit commitments on what you or others might do.

4. Don't let your access to power define your ego. Humility will earn you more respect and less resentment from those who do not have the same access to power.

5. Work on the matters that the Governor or you, and not everyone else, think are important.

6. Most written communications can become public records so have oral conversations, not written exchanges, about anything that you would not want to see as the lead on a news feed.

7. More than anything else, you get paid for your judgment. This requires seeing the five sides of every issue: legal, fiscal, political, social, and moral.

8. Chances are that a question that you are asked has been answered before. This means that your contacts may be faster and more informative than legal research.

9. Your Governor is not your state's first Governor. There are sound process and practices that previous Governors of both parties have used, especially for traditionally non-partisan matters like judicial selection and clemency reviews. At least understand them before advising a different course.

10. Identify the respected lawyers who preceded you as legal counsel and research their work product for guidance and templates.

11. Don't forget that you are practicing law. In addition to all of your policy work, you have ethical responsibilities tied to your license.

12. On important questions of law, particularly those involving power or authority, work hard to align with your Attorney General. But if you cannot get aligned and you think you are right, actively consider asking a court to opine.

13. You can't know everything you are asked. Admit it and don't speculate. Take the time to look it up and then answer.

14. Be loyal to your office colleagues, even the ones who are difficult. You are on the same team.

15. Keep relationships with an outside mentor or role model who can give you guidance, perspective, and moral support when the pressure builds.

B. Working with the Governor

1. Accept that the Legislature's plenary powers to enact, override, inquire and approve are greater than the Governor's supreme executive power.

2. Accept that the Governor's duty to faithfully execute the laws often means doing something less desirable unless or until you change that law. And understand that the Governor's executive orders can only go so far in closing that gap.

3. Understand the weighty difference between representation and leadership. Recognize when that distinction is at play, such as when facing a citizen initiative.

4. Recognize that many of the office's responsibilities are not ones of partisanship, but of non-partisan good governance and administrative practices.

5. Expect the Governor to be difficult at times. It is only with staff, a few close friends, and family that the Governor is out of public view and able to candidly vent the

frustrations that the pressure of the job and its unrelenting issues bring.

6. Always have possible answers to the problem you bring to the Governor for discussion or resolution.

7. The issue for the Governor is often not whether to support something, but whether to fund it.

8. Give the Governor the chance to sit with tough choices for a while. Difficult issues require multiple discussions to explore and extended time to consider. Plan when you will first raise and revisit such issues. Then prepare each discussion as the next opportunity to advance towards final decision.

9. Compromise is often not a capitulation of principle. It is the desired consequence of your constitution's intentional decision to divide power across and within branches.

10. Don't push important or complicated discussions with the Governor in between a slew of the Governor's other meetings. Reschedule.

11. Don't bring the Governor matters for decision when the Governor is tired, frustrated or otherwise not prepared for deliberative analysis. Reschedule.

12. Let the Governor vent when s/he needs to. Don't try to redirect the Governor until s/he has spoken and said their piece.

13. Deciding which bills to sign and which to veto is typically straightforward. But deciding which bills to let become law without signature is typically more difficult. Discuss with the Governor how s/he wants to define that standard.

14. Define the Governor's problems before your opponents do it for you.

15. Remind the Governor that there is a reason for the old expression about the press, which is never to pick a fight with people who buy ink by the barrel and paper by the ton. All the truer in the age of instant and constant internet news.

16. Find out what the Governor's "friends" who lobby, email, text and call her/him directly are discussing with the Governor. The advice they are providing may not be informed or selfless.

17. Advise the Governor and other top advisors to get out of the Capitol and its echo chamber regularly.

C. Working with Legislators

1. Make friends before you need them, especially with likely opponents and unlikely allies. Go up to the Legislature without any agenda item, see how people are doing, what is on their minds, and improve informal connections.

2. Don't get caught up in the merits of your own position. Understand and appreciate the other side's views.

3. Remember there is always tomorrow. Don't burn bridges or make unnecessary enemies.

4. Party affiliation is not legislators' only sense of identity. Legislators also identify across party lines as members of their house and of their Legislature. Do not pick fights that will coalesce those bi-partisan legislative identities against the executive.

5. Asking for input from legislators on issues makes them feel more like they are part of the exercise of power and less like they are on the receiving end of it.

6. When engaged with the legislative process, know exactly where you are procedurally. That will likely define your options.

7. Not every desire for a new law requires a novel approach. Look for analogues in existing law that may be applied.

8. Temper any frustration in working with legislators with the knowledge that serving as Governor's legal counsel will make a Hamiltonian out of anyone.

D. Decision-Making Processes

1. Start with recognizing that the threshold issue is not what gets decided. It's who gets to decide.

2. Make every decision as though you will have to explain it publicly.

3. Making decisions means not just what to decide, but how much to decide and when to decide it.

4. Anyone can issue spot. Your job is to identify the material issues and move them to a stable decision.

5. Use your legal training and experience to bring order and reason to the office's processes for making non-legal decisions.

6. Think always about the expert officials or affected constituency leaders who should be consulted for impact analysis prior to making decisions.

7. When making decisions with incomplete and evolving information, tell people that's what you're doing. Temper their expectations with the caveat that things can and likely will change.

8. Substantive answers are in the details, but the public explanation is in the sound bite. Distinguish—but connect—the two.

E. And Most Importantly …

1. Always remember what the constitution expressly assigns to you as your primary job: faithfully execute the laws.
2. On the tough days, and there will be many, take time to reflect on the true privilege of your opportunity to serve.

II.
The Basics of the Office

A. **Office Defined.** In Maine, the Office of Governor is defined by statute to include the Governor's Office, Governor's Office of Communications, *2 M.R.S. § 10;* Governor's Energy Office, *2 M.R.S. § 9;* Blaine House, *2 M.R.S. § 1; 3 M.R.S. § 162(12-A)* and *5 M.R.S. § 282-A(1)* and *§§ 321-326;* and Office of Policy Innovation and the Future, *5 M.R.S. §§ 3101-3107*. This book focuses solely on the Office of Governor.

B. **Election and Term.** The Governor is elected and re-elected "by plurality of all of the votes returned." *Art. V, Pt. 1, § 3.* Although rank-choice voting pursuant to *21-A M.R.S. § 723-A* applies to primaries for Governor, this constitutional requirement preempts the ranked-choice voting from applying to general or special elections for Governor. *Opinion of the Justices, 2017 ME 100 (2017)*. Once elected, the Governor serves a four-year term and may serve one second consecutive four-year term. *Art. V, Pt. 1, § 2.*

C. **Vacancy.** The Constitution intends continuous government, so the Office of Governor is always occupied. *Me. Atty. Gen. Ann. Rep. 1961-62 at 162-63*. Not even the interposition of the successor's oath is required because that would create a gap in occupancy. Opinion of the Justices, *70 ME 570, 592-94 (1880)*. Accordingly, the Constitution provides that whenever the office becomes vacant because of the death, resignation, or any other cause, *Art. V, Pt. 1, § 14* applies. Depending upon the circumstances, the Governor under *Art. V, Pt. 1, § 15* or the Legislature (after declaration by the Supreme Judicial Court and certification by the Secretary of State) under *Art. V, Pt. 1, § 14* may certify the office as vacant in the following scenarios:

1. **Temporary Incapacity.** Whenever the Governor is unable to discharge the powers and duties because of mental or physical disability, *Art. V, Pt. 1, § 15* applies.

2. **Continuous Incapacity for More than Six Months.** Whenever a Governor is continuously unable to discharge powers and duties for six months because of mental or physical disability, *Art. V, Pt. 1, § 14* applies.

3. **Removal.** A Governor may be removed only by impeachment; there is no recall provision. The House impeaches under *Art. IV, Pt. 1, § 8* and the Senate tries the articles of impeachment under *Art. IV, Pt. 2, § 7*. The Governor's powers of pardon do not reach those who have been impeached. *Art. V, Pt. 1, § 11*. For an elaboration on the subject of impeachment, see *The Federalist No. 65* and *Langhauser, History and Law of Presidential Impeachments, Maine PBS Broadcast, at https://www.pbs.org/video/understanding-the-president-trump-impeachment-process-jtq4oc/ (2020)*.

To date, 14 of Maine's 75 Governors left office before their term expired. Ten resigned primarily for health reasons or to take a federal position, and four died in office.

D. Succession. The order of succession to the Governor in the event of a vacancy is the Senate President, *Art. V, Pt. 1, § 14, ¶ 1*, House Speaker, *id. at ¶ 2*, and Secretary of State, *id. at ¶ 3*.

E. Compensation

1. **Salary and Allowances.** The Governor receives a "compensation, which shall not be increased or diminished during the Governor's continuance in office," *Art. V, Pt. 1, § 6;* an expense account, *2 M.R.S. § 2;* and a retirement allowance, *id.* at § 1-A.

2. **Blaine House.** The Governor is "entitled to reside in the Governor's official residence at Augusta during the Governor's term of office." *Id. at § 1.* Funding, repair, and restoration of the Blaine House are provided for by *3 M.R.S. § 162(12-A)* and *5 M.R.S. § 282-A(1), §§ 321-326*. The person who cares for the Blaine House is the private secretary referenced in *2 M.R.S. § 1.*

3. **Other.** The Governor must keep an office with regular hours and may keep the office desk and chair after serving. *Id.*

III.
Foundations of Executive and Related Powers

A. Power of the People

The power to make and change laws and elect officials is inherent in the people. *Me. Const. Art. I, Pt. 1, § 2 (hereinafter Art., Pt., §).* As regards lawmaking, this explains in whole the reason for the direct initiative provision of *Art. IV, Pt. 3, § 18,* and in part the reason for the referenda provision of *Art. IV, Pt. 3, § 17.* This fundamental lawmaking power of the people does not, however, extend to initiating constitutional amendments. *Art. X, § 4.*

B. Distribution and Separation of Powers

1. Governmental powers are distributed between the three branches of government and no branch may exercise the power of another. *Art. III, § 1 and § 2.* This prohibition in Maine is stricter than the federal analogue. *State v. Hunter, 447 A.2d 797 (Me. 1982).*

2. Governmental powers are separated into many hands in order to prevent the abuses that can come from aggregating too much power in too few hands. *See The Federalist Nos. 47-51.* There is both integration and separation in that distribution. The doctrines of bicameral enactment,

presentment, confirmation, and veto review require the separate actors, despite their separate powers, to work together through communication, cooperation and, ultimately, moderation. *Id.* This is the essence of the Madisonian model of American government.

3. One interesting Supreme Court case speaks in unusual terms about the duality of division and cooperation within the doctrine of separations. In *Plaut v. Spendthrift Farm, Inc., 514 U.S. 211 (1995)*, two Justices cited Robert Frost's poem, "Mending Wall," which describes two neighbors who each spring walk along a wall that separates their properties. One neighbor sees the spring walk as a chance to come together with his neighbor. The other sees the wall only for its function and symbolism: to separate himself from his neighbor. As applied to separations of power, Justice Breyer wrote that an important purpose of the doctrine is not just divide, but also to unite; to come and work together to find common interests. Justice Scalia, however, wrote that the purpose is simply to divide and, if the line of division is not clear, the parties will have the very problems they sought to avoid. *Id.*

4. On the one hand, the Governor needs to work with the legislative branch through the dynamics of bicameral enactment, presentment, confirmation, and veto review. On the other hand, the Governor must also be alert to legislative intrusions into executive power through bills that would infringe on the Governor's express constitutional powers, most commonly those enumerated in *Arts. III* and *V*, and as discussed *infra* throughout.

C. Nature of Legislative Power

The essence of legislative power is to "make and establish all reasonable laws and regulations for the defense and benefit of the people of this State, not repugnant to this Constitution, nor to that of the United States." *Art. IV, Pt. 3, § 1.* The Legislature has all power unless constrained by the Constitution. *SC Testing Technology, Inc. v. Dept. Environmental Protection, 688 A.2d 421 (Me. 1996); Ace Tire Co. v. Municipal Officers of Waterville, 302 A.2d 90 (Me. 1973); Sawyer v. Gilmore, 109 Me. 169 (1912).*

D. Nature of Executive Power

1. "The supreme executive power … shall be vested in a Governor." *Art. V, Pt. 1, § 1.* This provision creates the office of Governor and recognizes the Governor as the head of the executive department. *State v. Simon, 149 Me. 256 (1953); Opinion of Justices, 72 Me. 542 (1881).* This provision is not, however, the source of the Governor's power. The sections that follow contain specific grants of authority which comprise executive power. *Tinkle, The Maine State Constitution, at 114.*

2. The Executive has only the powers specifically conferred by the Constitution or the Legislature. *Opinion of the Justices, 72 Me. 542 (1881).* This includes all power specifically delegated or necessarily inferable from such delegations. *Id. at 546.*

3. The essence of executive power is to "take care that the laws be faithfully executed." *Art. V, Pt. 1, § 12.* Because faithful execution is the cornerstone of executive power, the subject is the focus of the next chapter.

4. For a thoughtful elaboration of the nature of executive power, *see The Federalist Nos. 69-70.*

E. Federal Limitations on State Power

1. There is the general federal supremacy of the laws of the United States: "The laws of the United States ... shall be the supreme law of the land; and the judges in every state shall be bound thereby, anything in the Constitution or laws of any State to the contrary notwithstanding." *U.S. Const. Art. VI, § 2.* This is the source of federal preemption in a number of areas, such as national labor relations. *29 U.S.C. §§ 151 et seq.; Opinion of the Justices, 571 A.2d 805 (Me. 1989)* (upholding Governor's decision to veto an enacted bill presented for approval that contravened this federal law because it violated the Supremacy Clause).

2. There are also the specific enumerated prohibitions on state power. These include, for example, laws that impair the obligation of contracts. *U.S. Const. Art. I, § 10 (¶ 1).* Congress also has specific enumerated powers that preempt the states. These include, for example, laws governing interstate commerce and copyright. *Id. at Art. I, § 8, (¶ 3) and (¶ 8).* Nonetheless, there is the residual grant that "powers not delegated to the United States by the Constitution, nor prohibited by it to the states, are reserved to the states respectively, or to the people." *Id. at Amend. X.* Examples of powers recognized as reserved to the states include creating public safety and school systems, managing trade and business within the state, and managing state courts and local government.

IV.
Faithful Execution

A. Introduction

The Constitution vests the "supreme executive power" of the State in the Governor. *Me. Const. Art. V, Pt. 1, § 1.* The Governor's constitutional role is, as conveyed by the terms "executive," "executive branch" and "executive powers," to "execute" the laws. "By definition, the chief executive in any constitutional system has this power, whether it is articulated or not. The framers of the Maine Constitution chose to make it explicit." *Tinkle, The Maine State Constitution, at 121.*

The power to execute the laws necessarily involves substantial discretion. To keep the Governor within the authority of the Office, the Constitution contains that discretion by imposing the duty to execute the laws "faithfully." And to reinforce this duty, the Constitution requires the Governor to take an oath to "faithfully discharge the duties" of the office. Together, these provisions impress upon the Governor a moral and affirmative duty to act diligently, honestly, skillfully, and impartially in the best interest of the public when implementing the laws. *See generally Kent, Leib & Shugerman, Faithful Execution and Article II, 132 Harv. L. Rev. 2111, 2141 (June 2019) (hereinafter Kent et al.).*

The essential task in faithful execution is to tether the interpretation of the law to an express or reasonably inferred meaning given the text, intent, and specific application of the law. When these elements are clear, the manner of execution will also be clear. But there is not always such clarity. Sometimes the text and/or intent are ambiguous or omissive, they may not fit a particular setting, or they may not account for an unforeseen development. Sometimes they may conflict with laws already in effect, or certain applications of the law will lead to unintended consequences. In these instances, reasonable interpretations will have to be developed, and in all instances biases for or against the policy advanced by the law will have to be moderated. For while there is discretion to bend execution in a preferred direction, the execution must still be grounded in reasonable readings of the text and intent in order to be "faithful."

B. Faithful Execution: Phrasing and Definitions

1. **Phrasing.** Rather than state directly that the Governor shall "faithfully execute the laws," the Constitution prescribes that the Governor shall "take care that the laws be faithfully executed." *Me. Const. Art. V, Pt. 1, § 12.* This choice of phrasing serves several purposes. First, it impresses a moral tone of care, attention, and protection. Second, it connotes that faithful execution is an affirmative, and not merely a responsive, duty. Because a core responsibility of executive power is to ensure the "steady administration of the laws," *The Federalist No. 70*, a Governor must actively take steps to ensure action on the front end and not wait to act until there is a complaint of inaction. And finally, the phrasing recognizes that most laws will be executed by executive branch employees other than the Governor. Here, the Governor's duty include superintending front-line executors to ensure that they act with faithfully as well. *Kent et al. at 2183.*

2. **Definitions.** The following definitions help inform the duty to "take care that the laws be faithfully executed."

   a. **"Take Care"** means to pay special attention to ensure that a command, duty, or trust is carried out. *Id. at 2134-35.*

   b. **"The Laws"** mean all measures and acts that have "the force of law," *accord Me. Me. Const. Art. IV, Pt. 3, § 2*, adopted "according to the Constitution and laws of the United States and the State of Maine." *Id. at Art. IX, § 1.* This includes the Constitutions of Maine and the United States, statutes enacted by Congress and the Legislature, regulations promulgated by state and federal agencies, state and federal court decisions interpreting such laws, and all other authorized governmental acts having the force of law.

   c. **"Faithfully"** means with diligence, care, trust, honesty, sincerity, truth, steadiness, and impartiality. It also means with strict adherence to duty, without failure of performance, with strong promises, and without fraud. *Kent et al. at 2132-33 (citing, among others, Noah Webster's and Samuel Johnson's Dictionaries).*

   d. **"Execute"** means to "finish, accomplish, make complete, fulfill, perform, or obey the terms of a command." *Black's Law Dictionary (2nd Ed. Online, 2023).* It also means to "to carry out fully; put completely into effect; do what is provided or required; carry out a design; or perform that which is required in order to give validity." *Merriam-Webster Dictionary (Online Ed., 2023).*

C. The Promissory Oaths

To buttress the duty of faithful execution, the Constitution requires the Governor to "take and subscribe" two oaths. *Me. Const. Art. IX, § 1.*

1. **Oath to Faithfully Discharge Duties.** The Governor must first swear to "faithfully discharge, to the best of my abilities, the duties incumbent on me … according to the Constitution and laws of the State." *Id.* Because a duty "incumbent upon [the Governor] according to the Constitution" is to "take care that the laws be faithfully executed," this second oath reinforces that command. Read together, the Governor must "faithfully discharge the duty to faithfully execute." This redundancy underscores the moral imperative of the obligation.

2. **Oath to Support the Constitutions**. The Governor must also swear to "support the Constitution of the United States and of this State, so long as I … shall continue a citizen thereof." *Id.* This oath is, fundamentally, a commitment to the rule of law, and it is "really a requirement of all federal and state offices, whether or not the office's organic law—the Constitution or statute—declares as much." *Prakash, Faithless Execution, 133 Harv. L. Rev. 94, 96 (2020).* Interestingly, the duration of this pledge is not just for the term of office but for the time of citizenship.

These oaths are not a mere formality. At the nation's founding, oath-swearing was as a "solemn and momentous event with real binding power over men's souls and hence their actions as well[,] … the safest knot of civil society, and the firmest band to tie all men to the performance of their several duties." *Kent et al. at 2124 and 2128 (citations omitted).* Indeed, to underscore the seriousness of purpose, the Governor must swear these oaths "in the presence of both Houses of the Legislature;" that is, before those who make the laws that the Governor is entrusted to execute faithfully. *Me. Const. Art. IX, § 1.*

And, unless the Governor conscientiously prefers an alternative affirmation, the oaths are to be sworn before God as well. *Id.*

D. Concepts Underlying Faithful Execution

Two prominent concepts that underlie the doctrine of faithful execution are the commitment to the rule of law and a fiduciary obligation to the electors.

1. **Commitment to the Rule of Law.** The framers of the United States and State of Maine Constitutions alike embraced the principle that it is only by rule of law that a society can best order itself to "establish justice, insure tranquility, provide for our mutual defense, promote our common welfare, and secure to ourselves and our posterity the blessings of liberty." *Me. Const. Preamble.* As the United States Supreme Court recognized very early in the life of our nation, ours is a "government of laws, and not of men." *Marbury v. Madison, 5 U.S. 137, 163 (1803).*

2. **Fiduciary Obligations to the Electors.** From "Plato through Cicero and Locke," the idea of public offices as trusts with fiduciary obligations has been embedded in "our constitutional tradition," and faithful execution has been called a "substantial textual and historical commitment" to these obligations. *Kent et al. at 2119.* Consider the observation by an anti-federalist at the time of federal constitutional ratification that elected representatives are:

   > the trustees of the people, the constitution the deed of gift, wherein they stood seized to ... only ... those uses being named, they cannot depart from them; but for their due performance are accountable to those by whose conveyance the trust was made. The right is therefore fiduciary, the power limited . . .

   Id. at 2182, citing in fn. 418 A Citizen of the State of Maryland, Remarks Relative to a Bill of Rights,

> *reprinted in 17 The Documentary History of the Ratification of the Constitution 91-2 (Kaminski & Saladino eds., 1988).*
>
> It is informative to note that the word "fiduciary" is derived from the Latin "fides," meaning "faith," and from "fiducia," meaning "in trust" or a "position of trust" or "confidence." *Kent et al. at 2119.* Accordingly, the basic obligations of a fiduciary are to be diligent, careful, honest, impartial, to not act outside of one's authority, and to not misuse or misappropriate funds or property. These prescriptions are of course apt for any public official, whether elected or appointed.

E. Broad Discretion but with Limits

Faithful execution is a principled but inexact standard that admits broad discretion. But as has been aptly noted, the "duty to fight fires does not necessarily suggest a power to purchase a fire truck." *Prakash at 98.* To that end, there are several concepts that limit the executive's discretion, the common theme being that faithful execution requires adherence to the prescriptions and intent of the lawmakers, so waivers or refusals to implement that direction without alternative authority is inconsistent with that obligation.

1. **There is No Power Not to Execute**. Execution is not just a power, it is also a duty; a duty that, as the United States Supreme Court has said of the President, defeats any claim of an implied or inherent power *not* to execute.

   > It was urged at the bar that the Postmaster General was alone subject to the direction and control of the President, with respect to the execution of the duty imposed upon him by this law, and this right of the President is claimed as growing out of the obligation imposed upon him by the Constitution to take care

> that the laws be faithfully executed. This is a doctrine that cannot receive the sanction of this Court... .
>
> To contend that the obligation imposed on the President to see the laws faithfully executed implies a power to forbid their execution is a novel construction of the Constitution, and entirely inadmissible... .
>
> It would be vesting in the President a dispensing power which has no countenance for its support in any part of the Constitution, and is asserting a principle which, if carried out in its results to all cases falling within it, would be clothing the President with a power entirely to control the legislation of Congress and paralyze the administration of justice.

Kendall v. United States ex Rel. Stokes, 37 U.S. 524, 612-13 (1838), cited with approval by Texas v. Biden, 20 F.4th 928, 981 (2021). Accord also United States v. Midwest Oil Co., 236 U.S. 459, 505 (1915); and United States v. Smith, 27 F. Cas. 1192 (C.C.D.N.Y. 1806).

2. **Execution Cannot Effectively Make New Law.** The executive was designed in the American scheme of constitutional law to be limited to defined delegations of executive authority. *See The Federalist Nos. 48 and 69* and historical sources cited in *Kent et al. at 2128-29.* Accordingly, executions that do not tie back to a delegation effectively make new law and thereby usurp the legislative power. Again, as the United States Supreme Court has said of the President, that there are no inherent or implied powers that are not executive in character.

> The contention is that presidential power should be implied from the aggregate of his powers under the Constitution. Particular reliance is placed on provisions in Article II which say that "The executive

> Power shall be vested in a President . . ."; that "he shall take Care that the Laws be faithfully executed" . . . . In the framework of our Constitution, the President's power to see that the laws are faithfully executed refutes the idea that he is to be a lawmaker. The Constitution limits his functions in the lawmaking process to the recommending of laws he thinks wise and the vetoing of laws he thinks bad. And the Constitution is neither silent nor equivocal about who shall make laws which the President is to execute.

Youngstown Sheet & Tube Co. v. Sawyer, 343 U.S. 579, 587 (1952).

3. **Execution Cannot Effectively Suspend the Law.** The Maine Constitution expressly provides that the laws shall "be in force, until altered or repealed by the Legislature, or shall expire by their own limitation," *Me. Const. Art. X, § 3*, and the laws "shall not be suspended but by the Legislature or its authority." *Id. at Art. I, § 13*. There are two ways—one by intentional action and the other by substantial inaction—that an execution may be claimed to have suspended laws.

Regarding intentional action, the prohibition has deep historical roots. In early English history, English Kings asserted as a "royal prerogative" the power to suspend a law by setting aside its operation for a time without actually repealing it. *Texas v. Biden, 20 F.4th at 979.* The English Bill of Rights and Liberties in 1689, however, rejected the idea that governing authority "inheres in the king by virtue of his kingship" and embraced instead the more democratic principle that such authority comes from a delegation by law. *Id. at 978-81*. In 1791, the Framers of the United States Constitution agreed. And in 1820, so did the Framers of the Maine Constitution when they expressly prohibited a Governor from unilaterally suspending the laws. *Me. Const. Art. I, § 13.*

Regarding substantial inaction, the prohibition goes to the core of the executive's duty. A Governor who earnestly objects to a policy underlying a law may be tempted to simply not to enforce it. But when such inaction rises to the level of essentially abandoning the law, such abdication can be tantamount to a suspension. *Accord, Texas v. Biden, 20 F.4th at 982-84.*

4. **Execution Cannot Effectively Dispense with the Law.** Another royal prerogative rejected by the English Bill of Rights and Liberties and the Federal and Maine Framers was the power to "dispense" with the law by granting permission to an individual or a corporation to disobey a statute. *Id. at 979.* The Maine Constitution likewise confers no such power of dispensation. The closest analogue is the power to "remit after conviction all forfeitures and penalties, and to grant reprieves, commutations and pardons." *Me. Const. Art. V, § 11.* But this is only "after conviction" and therefore only after the law has been executed.

5. **Execution Can Accommodate Case-Specific Prosecutorial Discretion.** Courts distinguish the above unconstitutional suspensions or dispensations of the law from lawful exercises of case-specific prosecutorial discretion. Under long-established common law, the executive may decide in individual applications of the law whether to enforce against a given person under specific circumstances at a particular moment in time. *Accord, Texas v. Biden, 20 F.4th at 983-84.* The authority to make these decisions is deemed to be a necessary attribute of individualized justice. Under faithful execution, the executive can exercise such prosecutorial discretion provided its case specific. Flouting a statutory command on a generalized, prospective basis to an

entire class of people has the practical effect of nullifying or suspending the whole statute. *Id.*

6. **Execution Must Effectively Serve the Public Interest.** Finally, some degree of political self-interest must be expected to motivate executive action because Governor is an elective office and "political self-interest is baked into the constitutional design." *Kent, Faithful Execution of the Office and Laws: New Research on the Original Meaning of Article II at https://www.lawfaremedia.org/article/faithful-execution-office-and-laws-new-research-original-meaning-article-ii (Oct. 10, 2018) (hereinafter Kent).* Yet balanced against this expectation is the moral principle that faithful execution imposes a duty to act "in good faith for the public interest ... and not for private profit, self-protection or other self-interested motives" that constitute self-dealing. *Kent et al. at 2141 and 2179.*

F. Common Challenges and Responses

As noted above, reasonable questions about how to execute a given law often arise. Poor text, unclear intent, inadequate resources, and legal problems in the law itself can all raise uncertainties. The following are common examples of such challenges and the approaches that a Governor may take.

1. **Textual Problems.** A Governor's job is to follow the instructions, authorizations, limitations, and prohibitions set forth by the Legislature. *Kent et al. at 2120.* But sometimes these are not clear. Undefined terms, ambiguous standards, imprecise meanings, incomplete schemes, conflicting references, and unclear intent cloud the picture. As a general rule of construction, laws are interpreted to authorize not only their express commands but also those meanings that are reasonably or necessarily inferable therefrom. *Accord, Opinion of the Justices, 72 Me. 542, 546 (1881) (applying the same rule of construction to the*

Governor's execution of powers). A statute that lacks clarity will require a deeper search for reasonable implications or inferences to ameliorate the omission, defect, or conflict in order to otherwise implement the law.

For bills that pose execution problems and have been presented but not yet acted upon by the Governor, a Governor can veto the bill under *Me. Const. Art. IV, Pt. 3, § 2* or request that it be recalled pursuant to *Mason's Manual of Legislative Procedure, R. 753 (3).* Once the bill becomes law, the Governor may provide gap-filling measures through a reasonable Executive Order *(see Chapter XI, infra)*, propose gap-filling regulations pursuant to *5 M.R.S. Ch. 375 (Administrative Procedures Act)*, propose a statutory amendment for corrective text, or a request for additional resources from the Legislature pursuant to *Me. Const. Art. V, § 9.* Steps such as these can be both legal and political evidence of good faith attempts at execution in unclear circumstances.

2. **Resource Shortages.** It is common for a Legislature not to provide the levels funding, staff positions, or purchase authority necessary for the executive to actualize fully the intent of the law. *Kent et. al. at 2185-86.* In these instances, the Governor may attempt a limited interim execution, perhaps with an interim Executive Order or temporary rule, until additional resources that would enable a fuller execution can be requested from the Legislature pursuant to *Me. Const. Art. V, Pt. 1, § 9.*

3. **Legal Questions.** Often a new enactment unwittingly conflicts with another existing state or federal law. To address these conflicts, the Governor may request an Opinion of the Attorney General pursuant to *5 M.R.S. § 195*, Opinion of the Justices pursuant to *Me. Const. Art. VI, § 3*, or a declaratory judgment pursuant to *14 M.R.S. Ch. 707.* Requests for a judicial opinion may be

particularly desirable if the legal question is constitutional. Scholars and activists debate the degree to which the oath to "support the Constitution[s]" is a grant of "departmentalism;" that is, the power of an executive as the head of the Executive Branch to decide the meaning of the Constitution to that branch. *See, for example, Kent et al. at 2186.* It can therefore be helpful to have a Governor's legal judgment buttressed by the opinion of an Attorney General, the Justices, or a lower court judge.

G. External Checks on Faithful Execution

There are several external sources of authority that can be used to check the executive's judgement on execution.

1. **Courts.** For questions of law, courts can be asked to enjoin, command, or penalize certain executive actions. Whether a court will act will depend on the degree to which the question is one of power, discretion, or ministerial action. *See Ch. VIII, § C.*

2. **Federal Agencies.** The Federal government can withhold the allocation of pertinent federal funds to a non-compliant State. The basic theory here is typically one of contract; that the State's form of execution or non-execution violates the conditions necessary for the State to continue to receive the federal monies. *See, for example, Mayhew v. Burwell, No. 14–1300 (1st Cir. Nov. 2014).*

3. **Legislature.** The Legislature has numerous tools and options to address execution issues. It can hold hearings and generate press to create political pressure on the executive to change its in/action. It can deny confirmation of a pertinent executive nominee or deny pertinent funding related to the in/action. It can hold other legislative initiatives hostage or ask the Attorney General or court to opine adversely on the executive's in/action. It can pass a

resolution decrying the executive in/action. It can pass a statute to defeat the executive in/action and, if necessary, override any veto of any such statute.

In severe cases, the Legislature can impeach a Governor for bad-faith execution of public office in violation of the Governor's oath. *Me. Const. Art. IV, Pt. 1, § 8 and Pt. 2, § 7.* As Gerald Ford once famously remarked, an impeachable offense is "whatever [a House majority] considers it to be at a given moment in history," and failing to comport or conduct oneself appropriately in public office is a "high misdemeanor" within the meaning of impeachment. *See Langhauser at https://www.pbs.org/video/understanding-the-president-trump-impeachment-process-jtq4oc/ (2020).* Indeed, in the three presidential impeachments between 1998 and 2020, each case charged violations, not of statutes, but of oaths of office. Transgressions of the duty of fidelity—as moralistic and subjective as it may be—were deemed worthy by a House majority in each case to merit a trial for removal from office.

4. **The People.** Finally, the people have several ways to express their concerns with one's perceived faithfulness to office. These include ballots for re-election *(Me. Const. Art. V, Pt. 1, § 2)*, votes on referenda *(id. at Art. IV, Pt. 3, § 17)*, and votes on citizen initiatives *(id. at § 18)*, where the issue may be presented in any one of a number of ways.

V.
Lawmaking and the Legislature

A. Governor's Powers and Duties

As regards lawmaking and the Legislature, the Governor's principal powers and duties are to:

1. **Swear In Legislators.** The Governor administers oaths to all legislators. *Art. IX, § 1.* In the event that the Governor is not able to swear a legislator, the chief or an associate justice of the Supreme Judicial Court may do so. *Id.*

2. **Address the Legislature.** "The Governor shall from time to time give the Legislature information of the condition of the State ... as the Governor may judge expedient." *Art. V, Pt. 1, § 9.* This is the origin of the State of the State Address.

3. **Propose Legislation.** "The Governor shall from time to time ... recommend to [the Legislature's] consideration such measures, as the Governor may judge expedient." *Id.* This means that the Governor is not subject to the Legislature's cloture deadline for submitting legislation.

4. **Present Enacted Bills.** "Every bill or resolution, having the force of law, to which the concurrence of both Houses may be necessary, ... which shall have passed both Houses,

shall be presented to the Governor." *Art. IV, Pt. 3, § 2.* Measures like bills and bond issues that define legal rights or assign legal duties have the force of law and require presentment. *Opinion of the Justices, 571 A.2d 1169 (Me. 1989)*; *Moulton v. Scully, 111 Me. 428, 448 (1914).* Legislative sentiments and the like that are mere instruments of communication do not require presentment.

5. **Approve or Allow Enactors.** The power to approve is exercised either by signing or not vetoing a bill within 10 days of presentment. *Art. IV, Pt. 3, § 2.* The rational for a time-limited law-without-signature option is twofold. First, to deny a Governor the power to thwart legislative action by the Governor's own inaction. And second, to serve the "demands of efficiency and convenience, of both legislative and executive officers" by imposing a 10-day limit and a clear default consequence. *Sutherland, Statutory Construction, § 16:3 (7th Ed.).*

6. **Disapprove Enactors.** The power to disapprove is exercised in three ways.

   a. **General Veto.** For any measure that has the force of law (excluding per *Art. IV, Pt. 3, § 18* citizen initiatives), the Governor must return a vetoed bill to the chamber of its prime sponsor within 10 days of presentment (starting the day after the bill comes down). *Art. IV, Pt. 3, § 2.* To override a veto, the Legislature must have a two-thirds (present) vote in both chambers. Stated differently, to sustain a veto the Governor only needs a one-third (present) vote in one chamber. *Id.*

   The Governor's veto power does not extend to citizen's initiatives or constitutional amendments approved by the Legislature before either is sent to the people. *Art. IV, Pt. 3, § 18(2)* and *Art. X, § 4.*

For a thoughtful elaboration of the general veto power, *see The Federalist No. 73.*

b. Line-Item Veto. The line-item veto power is in addition to, and does not replace, the Governor's general veto power. If the Governor does not issue a line-item veto within one day of presentment, the Governor still has nine days within presentment to issue a general veto. *Opinion of the Justices, 673 A.2d 1291 (Me.1996).* The line-item veto works very differently from the general veto.

Within one day of presentment, the Governor may disapprove any dollar amount appearing in an appropriation or allocation section of an enacted bill. *Art. IV, Pt. 3, § 2-A.* For any disapproved amount, the Governor must:

(1) replace the dollar amount with one that does not increase an appropriation or allocation or decrease a de-appropriation or deallocation;

(2) not propose an increase in an appropriation or allocation elsewhere in the bill; and

(3) not disapprove, omit, or modify any statutory or unallocated language. *Id.*

Each dollar amount vetoed is then voted on separately, with only a simple majority of all elected members of each house required to override each line-item veto. *Id.*

c. Pocket Veto. A pocket veto can occur only at the end of a second regular session when the Governor has not signed or returned a bill; the Legislature adjourns prior to the expiration of the Governor's 10-day signing period; and the Legislature does not return for at least three consecutive days prior to the end of that Legislature. *Art. IV, Pt. 3, § 2.* If the Legislature does come back into a special session, the Governor on the fourth day must then deliver a veto message to the chamber of origin or the bill becomes law.

7. **Decision Whether to Approve, Allow, or Disapprove Enactors.** In deciding which of the three actions to take on a presented bill, a Governor typically:

   a. **Signs a Bill** when the Governor affirmatively supports or does not have consequential reasons to oppose it.

   b. **Vetoes a Bill** when the Governor opposes it because of consequential policy, legal, financial, or political reasons.

   c. **Allows a Bill to Become Law without Signature** when the Governor is indifferent to it (for example, does not think the bill is necessary or impactful but is not otherwise harmful), or is mindful of any one of a number of factors, such as:

      (1) the breadth of legislative or public support for the bill;

      (2) the bill is better than a previous effort that was vetoed, or letting the bill become law otherwise ends a long-standing political debate;

      (3) there will be opportunities for the legislature to improve the bill in a subsequent session;

      (4) there are executive actions (such as regulations, executive orders, or enforcement strategies) that can mitigate the adverse impacts of the bill;

      (5) there may be court action that could affect the validity or impact of the law; and/or

      (6) although the Governor's concerns do not rise

to the level of expending the political capital necessary to sustain a veto, the Governor wants nonetheless to "call definite attention" (in the words of President Franklin D. Roosevelt) to the fact that the executive did not support the bill. *Accord, Philip Buchen, Enactment of Legislation Without the Approval of the President, White House Counsel Memorandum at 3 (Sept. 13, 1976) at https://www.fordlibrarymuseum.gov/library/document/0019/4520478.pdf* (also providing an informative account of the presidential power under federal law).

8. **Recall of Legislation.** The Legislature, typically by joint order, may request to recall from the Governor an enacted bill presented for signature. *Mason's Manual of Legislative Procedure, R. 753(3).* Recall can be a helpful way to avoid vetoes and unnecessary fights over fixable problems. But the Legislature cannot compel the Governor to so return a bill, and the Governor cannot compel the Legislature to make such a request.

B. Lawmaking Need-to-Know Short List

Amid the myriad of rules governing lawmaking, these are the more noteworthy.

1. Legislative Sessions

a. Regular Sessions

(1) By statute, the first regular session is supposed to adjourn by the third Wednesday in June, and the second regular session by the third Wednesday in April. *3 M.R.S. § 2.*

(2) The Legislature may, however, by a vote of 2/3 of the members of each house present and voting

extend the date for adjournment of either session by up to five legislative days, and by the same votes extend for five additional legislative days. *Id.*

(3) The times for adjournment for the first and second regular sessions may also be extended for one additional legislative day to consider vetoes. *Id.*

b. Special Sessions

(1) The Legislature can call itself into special session only with the approval of the speaker, the president and majority of each political party. *Art. IV, Pt. 3, § 1.*

(2) The Governor may convene a special session of the Legislature whenever the Governor chooses. *Art. V, Pt. 1, § 13.* The Legislature cannot mandate that the Governor convene a special session, *Op. Me. Atty. Gen. (Ap. 2, 1980).* The Governor alone determines the necessity for convening the Legislature, and this decision is not subject to review. *Opinion of Justices, 136 Me. 531 (1940).* The Governor may revoke a proclamation convening the Legislature and issue a new proclamation convening the Legislature to another date certain. *Id.*

2. **Stages of the Legislative Process.** It is essential to have a solid understanding of the parliamentary tools available for use at each stage of the legislative process: drafting, printing, referral to committee, committee hearing, work session, report, first reading, second reading, engrossment, and enactment. For a summary of this process, *see*

Legislator's Handbook, pp. 2-14, at https://Legislature.maine.gov/doc/2611; and *Joint Rules* discussed therein.

3. **Emergency vs. Non-Emergency Legislation.** Emergency bills take effect when signed (or a veto is overridden) and require a 2/3 vote of "all the members elected to each House." *Art. IV, Pt. 3, § 16.* The required vote is 2/3 of the entire membership, not 2/3 of those present and voting. *Opinion of the Justices, 230 A.2d 802 (Me. 1967).* Non-emergency bills take effect 90 days after the enacting Legislature adjourns *sine die* and require only a simple majority of those present and voting. *Id.*

4. **Other Super-Majority Requirements.** Certain legislative measures (i.e., emergency bills noted above and bonds) and legislative actions (i.e., overrides and confirmations) require a super-majority of 2/3. When a super-majority is required, the baseline varies between 2/3 of the full elected membership of each house and 2/3 of those legislators present and voting. For example:

   a. **Full Elected Membership.** State mandates on local government require 2/3 of the full elected membership. *Art. IX, § 21.*

   b. **Present and Voting.** For example:

      (1) Override a veto, *Art. IV, Pt. 3, § 2;*

      (2) Overturn a committee confirmation recommendation, *Art. V, Pt. 1, § 8;*

      (3) Enact a bond issue, *Art. IX, § 14;* and

      (4) Amend a constitutional amendment, *Art. X, § 4.*

For a helpful quick reference, see the 2/3 vote summary chart on the following page.

Noteworthy Legislative Actions Requiring 2/3 Votes

2/3 of the Full Elected Membership

Subject	Votes Required		Source
Emergency Measure	101 House /24 Senate		Art. IV, Pt. 3, § 16
State Mandate	101 House /24 Senate		Art. IX, § 21
State Park Land	101 House /24 Senate		Art. IX, § 23
Mining Excise Tax Trust Fund	101 House /24 Senate		Art. IX, § 20
State Constitutional Convention	101 House /24 Senate Concurrently		Art. IV, Pt. 3, § 15
2/3 of Legislators Present and Voting			
Bond Issue	2/3 Present & Voting		Art. IX, § 14
Veto Override	2/3 Present & Voting		Art. IV, Pt. 3, § 2
Constitutional Amendment	2/3 Present & Voting		Art. X, § 4
Reapportionment Plans	2/3 Present & Voting		Art. IV, Pt. 1, § 3; Art. IV, Pt. 2, § 2
Impeachment Conviction	2/3 Present & Voting		Art. IV, Pt. 2, § 7
Expel a Member	2/3 Present & Voting		Art. IV, Pt 3, § 4
Overturn Confirmation Com. Rec.	2/3 Present & Voting		Art. V, Pt. 1, § 8
Confirmation Process Change	2/3 Present & Voting		Art. V, Pt. 1, § 8
Remove Disabled Governor	2/3 Present & Voting	in Jt. Conv.	Art. V, Pt. 1, § 14
U.S. Constitutional Convention	2/3 Present & Voting		Jt. Rule 215 (1)
Amend or Suspend Rule	2/3 Present & Voting		Jt. Rules 102-03
Reintroduce Defeated Measure	2/3 Present & Voting		Jt. Rule 217
Recall Item from Legislative Files	2/3 Present & Voting		Jt. Rule 404

5. **Usurpation.** Bills can both intentionally and unintentionally interfere with the Governor's powers. Such bills constitute an unconstitutional usurpation of executive power in violation of separation of powers. *Art. III, § 1* and *§ 2.* Often subtle but recurring examples include bills that interfere with the Governor's pardon and commutation, appointment, and proposal powers.

6. **Delegation.** Legislatures occasionally seek to shift power away from the executive by delegating authority to independent agencies or other entities directly overseen by a board and not the Governor. Lawful delegations must include minimal meaningful standards for guiding the exercise of such authority and should have a mechanism of ultimate accountability to an elected, as opposed to an appointed, official. *See generally 29 Journal of College & University Law 1 (2002).*

7. **Cannot Bind a Successor Legislature.** It is common for Legislatures to attempt to impose standards that cannot be changed by future Legislatures. A Legislature can, however, only legislate for its elected term and cannot bind a successor Legislature. *SC Testing Technology, Inc. v. Dept. Environmental Protection, 688 A.2d 421 (Me. 1996); Opinion of the Justices, 673 A.2d 693 (Me. 1996); Me. Op. Atty Gen. 89-12.*

8. **Confirmation of Nominations.** The processes for posting, hearing, and voting of appointees requiring senate confirmation are summarized in *Chapter XII.* As regards approval or confirmation of nominees, a nominee first needs a simple majority vote of a quorum of committee members present and voting. *Art. V, Pt. 1, § 8; Joint Rule 505 of the 130th Legislature.* The committee's recommendation then becomes final unless it is overridden by a vote of 2/3 of the Senators present and voting. *3 M.R.S. § 158.*

This mechanism—using a floor supermajority to negate a committee action—is rare.

9. **Cannot Appoint Sitting Legislators.** During their term of office, no legislator can be appointed to a compensated position that requires legislative approval for appointment, or that has been created or had a pay raise approved during that term. *Art. IV, Pt. 3, § 10.*

10. **Citizen Initiatives.** Although ours is a representative democracy, the people have reserved to themselves the right to legislate themselves directly. The detailed processed for proposing a question, gathering signatures, having legislative review, and voting at the polls is set forth in *Art. IV, Pt 3, §18*. These are often fueled more by passionate advocacy than dispassionate reason. Citizen initiatives are statutory in nature, so they may be subsequently amended or repealed if there is legislative and gubernatorial will. *See, for example, Langhauser, Legislative Amendment of Citizen Initiatives: Where the "Will of the Voter" Meets the "Consent of the Elector," Me. Pol. Rev. 30.1 (2021).*

11. **Adapting Existing Doctrines to New Questions.** Every new bill is a proposed remedy to a perceived new problem. As noted in Maxim C (7) in *Chapter I* above: "Not every question for a new law requires a novel approach. Look for analogues in existing law that may be applied." This can be a very effective approach. See, for example, the statutes to restrict firearm possession for persons in crisis based on principles of protective custody (*P.L. ch. 411 (2019*); to require adult involvement in minors' access to abortions based on principles of informed consent *(22 M.R.S.A. § 1597-A (1989));* and to protect military funerals from protests based on principles from RICO and copyright statutes as well as diverse free speech opinions *(P.L. 112–154, § 601 (2012).*

12. **Legislative Reapportionment Plan.** Legislative reapportionment plans for House, Senate, Congressional, and County Commissioner districts are subject to the Governor's approval. *Art. IV, Pt. 1, § 3; Art. IV, Pt. 3, § 2; Art IX, §§ 24* and *25.*

VI.
Public Integrity

A. Background. A wide variety of statutes impose detailed duties related to public integrity. Note that the Law Court has, in construing *Art. V, § 10* (requiring information from officers), spoken in somewhat contradictory terms. In the same opinion, the Court observed first that any matter that is properly before any executive office may be considered pending before the Governor, even if the Governor has no direct authority over it. *State v. Simon, 149 Me. 256 (1953).* But then the Court recognized the reality that the "varying degrees of detailed conduct in the executive business of the state" clearly lies with other executive branch employees. *Id.*

B. Improper Influence

1. There are at least eight criminal statutes covering "bribery and corrupt practices" that prohibit a Governor (and all public servants) from soliciting, accepting, or agreeing to accept any pecuniary benefit in return for a decision, opinion, recommendation, nomination, vote, or other official act. *17-A M.R.S. §§ 602-609* (elements and scienter are set forth in each offense).

2. Maine law also prohibits and limits the Governor and the Governor's staff from soliciting or accepting certain contributions when the Legislature is in session, *1 M.R.S. § 1015-A(2)*, and not in session. *Id. at § 1015-A(3).*

3. Likewise, certain other executive employees are prohibited from using their official authority, influence, or supervisory position for the purpose of attempting to influence another's partisan political contribution or participation. *5 M.R.S. § 7056-A.*

C. **Financial Disclosure.** The Governor must annually file with the Commission on Governmental Ethics and Election Practices a statement identifying the sources of income received, positions held, and reportable liabilities incurred during the preceding calendar year by the Governor and members of the Governor's immediate family. *Id. at § 19.* Certain other executive (typically policymaking) employees are required to disclose annually certain personal and immediate family financial information. *See generally id.* (Executive employees) and *id. at § 931(1)(G)* (Governor's office employees).

D. **Conflicts of Interest.** One statute disqualifies executive employees from working on certain matters depending upon their prior state employment. *5 M.R.S. § 18.* Another prohibits conflicts of financial interest for self and immediate family, including but not limited to approving certain contracts. *Id. at § 18-A.* There is also the federal prohibition on state employees, whose principal duties are connected to an activity financed in part by federal funds, running for partisan political office during their terms of service. *5 U.S.C. § 1501 et seq.* (Hatch Act). Note further that, by comparison, legislators have their own code of ethics regarding conflict of interest. *1 M.R.S. § 1011 et seq.*

E. Acceptance of Gifts. Only the Governor may accept, or delegate acceptance of, gifts given to the state. *2 M.R.S. § 5.* The Governor also accepts on behalf of the state federal funds for public broadcasting, *20-A M.R.S. § 851,* and gifts to the Maine International Trade Center, *10 M.R.S. § 495-I.*

The Governor's acceptance of personal gifts is governed by the corruption, conflicts, and disclosure laws cited above. And the ability to lawfully accept gifts is in part defined by the *de minimus* exception in the Criminal Code when the gift and circumstances are "within a customary license or tolerance, not inconsistent with the purpose of the law, did not actually cause or threaten the harm sought to be prevented by the law, or did so only to an extent too trivial to warrant the condemnation of conviction." *17-A M.R.S. §12(1).*

F. Freedom of Access. The Freedom of Access Act (FOAA) is a very broad law that applies to certain individuals and groups in the meetings they hold and the documents they produce. *See 1 M.R.S. § 401, et seq,* with meetings *at § 402(2)* and documents *at § 403(3).* There is an express presumption of access in *1 M.R.S. § 401* and categorical exceptions are in *§ 402(3).* Approximately 300 other exceptions are provided throughout the statutes. *Search at http://www.maineLegislature.org/legis/foa/.*

FOAA applies to the Governor's office, but several exceptions are noteworthy.

1. The Governor's cabinet meetings are not subject to the law. The cabinet is an informal collective, is not established by law, is not legally authorized to perform specific functions, and is purely advisory. *Accord* analyses of *Op. Me. Atty. Gen. 85-19* and *Rushforth v. Council of Economic Advisers, 762 F.2d 1038 (D.D.C. 1985).*

2. The proceedings and records of any authority, board, commission, committee, council, task force or similar organization of an advisory nature, established, authorized, or organized by an executive order issued by the Governor, provided such executive order specifically exempts the organization from FOAA. *1 M.R.S. § 402(1)(F).*

3. Certain personal information contained in a communication between a constituent and the Governor. *Id. at § 402(3)(C-1)(1).*

4. Certain personal contact information concerning Governor's office employees. *Id. at § 402 (3)(O).*

5. Information disclosed by a business that legitimately constitutes a trade secret pursuant to *10 M.R.S. § 1542(4)* and *M. R. Evid. 507.*

6. A Governor's proposed legislation if the draft is "used or maintained by any Legislator, legislative agency, or legislative employee … during the legislative session or sessions in which the papers or reports are prepared or considered," *1 M.R.S. § 402(3)(C).*

G. Record Retention

1. Maine law requires certain documents and records of the office to be retained for archives. *5 M.R.S. § 91 et seq.* The requirements and schedule for retention are set by regulation of the state archivist. *Id. at § 95-C.* The schedule for the Governor's office is accessible through *https://www.maine.gov/sos/arc/records/.*

2. The Secretary of State preserves all official acts and proceedings of the Governor. *Art. V, Pt. 2, § 4.* For example, copies of executive orders, proclamations, and clemency warrants are sent to and retained by the Secretary of State.

3. It is a Class E crime to knowingly violate the record retention laws, *5 M.R.S. at § 97;* a Class D crime to unlawfully destroy or tamper with an official record, *17-A M.R.S. § 456*; and a Class D crime to unlawfully remove, secrete, or mutilate a state document, *1 M.R.S. § 452.*

H. Audit. A post-audit of all accounts and other financial records of the Governor's office, except the Governor's Expense Account, shall be performed at least once every 2 years by independent certified public accountants designated by the Governor. *3 M.R.S. § 4.*

I. Governor-Elect's Transition Committee. The finances and activities of the Governor-elect and related transition committee are subject to *1 M.R.S. § 1051.*

VII.
Public Safety

A. National Guard

The Governor:

1. Is the "commander in chief of the army and navy of the State, and of the militia, except when the same are called into the actual service of the United States." *Art. V, Pt. 1, § 7.* This provision dovetails with the federal Constitution which reserves to the states the right to maintain their own militia. *U.S. Const. Art. I, § 8, cl. 16.* Note that the Governor may not withhold consent to training National Guard units outside the United States. *10 U.S.C. § 12301(f), upheld in 686 F. Supp. 30 (D. Mass. 1988) and affirmed in 859 F.2d 1066 (1st Cir. 1988).*

2. Shall "issue from time to time such orders and regulations and to adopt such other means of administration, as shall maintain the prescribed standard of organization, armament and discipline; and such orders, regulations and means adopted shall have the full force and effect of the law." *Art. VII, § 4.*

3. Appoints the adjutant general. *Art. VII, § 3.*

4. May activate the National Guard "in the case of, or imminent danger of, insurrection, invasion, tumult, riot, conspiracy to commit a felony or threat of violence to persons or property or upon the reasonable apprehension thereof; or for the safety of the inhabitants of this State; or, in the case of actual or imminent public disaster, to the aid of any civil authority." *37-B M.R.S. § 181-A(1).* Such conditions may or may not also be during a state of emergency under *id. at § 742.*

B. Disasters, Civil Emergencies, and Emergency Management

1. **Background.** On the one hand, the delegation of emergency powers is an extraordinary allocation that implies a particular trust and a careful respect for limited use. On the other hand, emergency management is an inherently practical exercise: there are fact-based problems that require prompt and effective responses. This means that the determination of the scope of any one of the Governor's emergency powers is not a conceptual analysis but a practical one. For this reason, the Governor's powers should be regarded as dynamically expansive depending on the circumstances.

2. **MEMA.** The Maine Emergency Management Agency (MEMA) performs essential functions that require a relatively thorough understanding prior to an actual emergency. *Id. at § 701 et seq.* The Governor and key staff should both be oriented and trained before an emergency arises.

3. Important Definitions

a. "Civil emergency" is not defined in the Maine Emergency Management Act, so it appears to be an umbrella term meant to capture events like those identified elsewhere, such as, for example, radiation hazards, *25 M.R.S. § 50;* insurrection, *37-B M.R.S. § 182*; forest fires, *12 M.R.S. § 9001*; and oil spills, *38 M.R.S. § 5470.*

b. Civil emergency includes "disasters" which is defined to mean "the occurrence or imminent threat of widespread or severe damage, injury or loss of life or property resulting from any natural or man-made cause, including, but not limited to, fire, flood, earthquake, wind, storm, wave action, oil spill or other water contamination requiring emergency action to avert danger or damage, epidemic, extreme public health emergency ..., air contamination, blight, drought, critical material shortage, infestation, explosion, riot or hostile military or paramilitary action." *37-B M.R.S. § 703(2).*

Note that, during the state shutdown in 1991, the failure to timely enact a state budget was deemed to be a "man-made ... threat of ... injury or loss of life or property." An emergency was proclaimed, and emergency powers were used to ensure the continuation of essential governmental services. *Me. Exec. Ords. 1-7 FY 90/91.*

4. Emergency Proclamations

a. The Governor *must* proclaim a state of emergency "whenever a disaster or civil emergency exists or appears imminent." *37-B M.R.S. § 742(1)(A).*

b. The Governor can only access emergency powers after a state of emergency is proclaimed. *Id.*

c. States of emergency proceed in 30-day increments, *id. at* § 743 and may be extended by such increments as long as deemed necessary.

d. A state of emergency is terminated by expiration of the 30 days, proclamation of the Governor, or termination by joint legislative resolve. *Id.*

e. Certain powers may be exercised for reasonably limited periods of time after the proclamation terminates because "recovery" is one of the four phases of emergency management expressly recognized by statute. *Id. at § 701(1)* and *§ 742(C)*. In the transition phase out of a state of emergency, the Governor may continue to coordinate, mitigate, and recover, where:

(1) "coordination" means coordinating "all emergency management and homeland security functions ... to the maximum extent with the comparable functions of the Federal Government, including its various departments and agencies, of other states and localities, and of private agencies so that the most effective preparation and use may be made of the nation's workforce, resources and facilities for dealing with any disaster that may occur." *Id. at § 702;*

(2) "Mitigation" means mitigating "those activities that actually eliminate or reduce the chance of occurrence or the effects of a disaster." *Id. at § 703(3-A);* and

(3) "Recovery" means supporting "activities that, in the short term, return vital life support systems to minimum operating standards and, in the long term, redevelop a disaster area to preexisting conditions or to conditions that are less disaster prone and activities that assist families and businesses to return to a normal or improved state of being." *Id. at § 703(6).*

For examples of specified acts authorized during a transition out of state of emergency, see *Me. Exec. Ord. 40 FY 20/21.*

5. **General and Specific Powers.** Key emergency powers under *37-B M.R.S.* §§ 741-742 include the authorities to:

   a. Make, amend, and rescind a necessary order or rule related to the emergency;

   b. Adjust a time frame or deadline imposed by law for state, county or municipal governments or other entity;

   c. Suspend the enforcement of a statute prescribing the procedures for conduct of state business;

   d. Suspend the enforcement of a statute, agency rule, agency regulation, agency order, or emergency rule that is inconsistent with emergency management and to the extent that the inconsistency exists;

   e. Modify or suspend the requirements for professional or occupational licensing or registration by any agency, bureau, board, or commission; and

   f. Take other action necessary to mitigate the danger of the emergency.

Drawing from other Maine laws, the Governor may also spend from the contingent account for emergency purposes, *5 M.R.S. § 1507 (4)*: exercise eminent domain powers, *37-B M.R.S. § 821;* and authorize emergency use of unmanned aerial vehicles, *25 M.R.S. § 4501(4)(G).*

Note finally that, for COVID, pandemic-specific powers were enacted just before the state of emergency was declared. *P.L. 2019, c. 617* enacting inter alia *37-B M.R.S. § 742(C)(13)(a-c).*

6. **Enforcement of Emergency Orders.** Violations of an emergency order constitute a Class E crime. *37-B M.R.S. § 786.*

7. **Litigation Precedent.** Courts have upheld the actions of Governors who have exercised their emergency powers with careful reasoning and authorizing citations.

   a. **Pandemic.** As regards the 2020-21 period of the pandemic, *see*, for example, *Bayley's Campground, Inc. v. Mills, 985 F.3d 153 (1st Cir. 2021)* (upholding Governor's exercise of COVID emergency powers as applied to restrictions affecting interstate travel and affirming *463 F. Supp. 3d 22 (D. Me. 2020))*; *Calvary Chapel of Bangor v. Mills, 984 F. 3d 21 (1st Cir. 2020)* (upholding Governor's exercise of COVID emergency powers as applied to restrictions affecting in-person faith services and affirming *459 F. Supp. 3d 273 (D. Me. 2020)* (cert denied in *142 S. Ct. 71 (2021))*; *Savage v. Mills, 478 F. Supp. 3d 16 (D. Me. 2020)* (dismissing 11-count omnibus challenge to Governor's exercise of COVID emergency powers and executive orders); and *Tiffany Bond v. Mills, 2020 WL 4275035 (D. Me. 2020)* (upholding Governor's exercise of COVID emergency powers as applied to restrictions affecting election candidate signature gathering).

   b. **Budget Shutdown.** As regards the 1991 budget shutdown, *see Bureau of Employee Relations v. Maine Labor Relations Board, CV-94-27 (Me. Sup. Ct., June 7, 1994), overruling Maine State Employees Association v. State of Maine, 92-19 (M.L.R.B., Jan. 6, 1994), and appeal dismissed, 655 A.2d 326 (Me. 1995)* (upholding Governor's exercise of emergency powers as applied to impact on state employees during budgetary shutdown of state government); and *Butterfield* *v. McKernan, CV-91-29 (Me. Super. Ct., Jan. 17, 1991)* (upholding during budget shortfall Governor's executive order curtailing approximately $53 million in previously authorized spending).

c. **Keys to Upholding Executive Actions.** Actions in both of the above emergencies were upheld in large part because the rationale for the actions was clearly stated in the proclamations and executive actions and detailed the specific authority(s) being exercised. For a recent example of such an order, see *Me. Exec. Ord. 57 FY 19/20.*

C. Guns

1. **Constitutional Right.** Maine citizens have a right to "keep and bear arms." *Art. I, § 16.*

2. **State Preemption.** The state occupies and preempts the entire field of legislation concerning the regulation of firearms, components, ammunition, and supplies. With limited exceptions, any existing or future order, ordinance, rule, or regulation in this field of any political subdivision of the state is void. *25 M.R.S. § 2011.*

3. **Prohibited Persons.** Certain persons lose their right to possess a firearm because of a criminal felony conviction, domestic violence offense, or mental health hospitalization. *15 M.R.S. § 393(1)-(1-B).* There is also a law that immediately restricts firearm possession for certain persons in crisis. *34-B M.R.S. § 3862-A.*

4. **Petition the Governor.** After five years, certain prohibited persons may petition the Governor for restoration of their rights. *15 M.R.S. § 393(2)-(4).* The Governor's authority here is delegated to the Commissioner of the Department of Public Safety, which has a long-established process for

notifying and seeking comment from courts and other interested parties when a restoration of the right to possess firearms is sought.

D. Protests at the Capitol

The Governor maintains offices in the Capitol and the Capitol attracts, as it should, many different citizens and activists. So an understanding of the following is informative.

1. **Control.** The Capitol is controlled by the legislative branch. The Legislature, and not the Governor, establish the rules for the Capitol. *25 M.R.S. § 2904.*

2. **Capitol Security.** The Maine State Police has the authority to safeguard persons and property in the State House and Capitol Area. *25 M.R.S. § 2904* and *16-219 C.M.R. Ch. 41 § 1(A).* The Capitol Area includes any "land, building, personal property, and facilities owned, leased, occupied, used, or possessed by the State … within the city limits of Augusta," including the State House, Cross State Office Building, DHHS Building, Blaine House Complex, and State Cultural Building. *16-219 C.M.R. Ch. 41 § 1(A)* and *1 M.R.S. § 814(2).*

3. **Permits.** No person shall cause or participate in a demonstration of any nature in the Capitol Area unless written permission for such demonstration has been obtained from the Commissioner of Public Safety or his Designee." *16-219 C.M.R. Ch. 41 § 2(B).* A person found guilty of violating a Capitol Area regulation may, upon conviction, be punished by a $50 fine. *Id. at § 3* applying *25 M.R.S. § 2910.*

4. **Protected Speech vs. Unlawful Conduct**

   a. **Lawful Expression.** The Capitol is in certain locations—such as the walkways outside and Hall of Flags and legislative hallways—a traditional public forum and, as such, receives broad speech protection under the First Amendment. Moreover, political speech, which is often that being exercised at the Capitol is a form of expression that also receives the highest protection under the First Amendment. *See, for example, Langhauser, Free and Regulated Speech on Campus: Using Forum Analysis for Assessing Facility Use, Speech Zones and Related Expressive Activity, 31 J. Col. & Univ. L. 481 (2005).*

b. **Unlawful Expression.** Speech that promotes or produces an unlawful end is not protected by the First Amendment. *Id.* This includes expression that promotes the imminent prospect of actual violence or harm, fighting words, terrorist threats, speech that constitutes or promotes gross disobedience of legitimate rules, harassment, defamation, obscenity, and criminal trespass. *Id.* Moreover, reasonable content-neutral limitations under forum analysis lawfully permit the enforcement of reasonable time (e.g., duration), manner (e.g., volume), and place (e.g., not in private offices) restrictions that are content neutral. *Id.* The keys in all cases are to give the speaker a reasonable opportunity to express her/himself, to distinguish speech from conduct, and to distinguish the content of speech from the effect (disruption, threatening) that such speech has on orderly operations of government. *Id.*

c. **Potential Consequences for Unlawful Expression.** Depending on the nature and severity of the conduct, criminal violations beyond the modest fine noted above may be implicated. These violations include, for example, conduct that constitutes criminal trespass, criminal threatening, disorderly conduct, obstructing government administration, aggravated/

criminal mischief, failure to disperse, riot, unlawful assembly, obstructing public ways, harassment, desecration, and defacement. *17 M.R.S. §§ 209-806.* These offenses range from Class C to Class E crimes with penalties of imprisonment, *17-A M.R.S. § 1604,* and more significant fines, *id. at* § 1704 (for individuals) and § 1705 (for organizations).

Finally, note that flag burning can be a form of political protest. Although a statute expressly prohibits openly mutilating or casting contempt upon the flag, *1 M.R.S. § 254*, the Law Court has upheld prosecutions of this statute only when the burning poses an actual and imminent threat of harm. *State v. Peacock, 138 Me. 339 (1942).*

5. **Governor's Authority.** To support Capitol Security in severe cases, the Governor may "order members of the state military forces to active state service in the case of, or imminent danger of, insurrection, invasion, tumult, riot, conspiracy to commit a felony or threat of violence to persons or property or upon the reasonable apprehension thereof ... " *37-B M.R.S. § 181-A(1).* As applied to the Capitol, this power implicates the constitutional requirements that the government remain continuous, *Art. IX, § 17,* and that, except in an emergency, Augusta shall be the seat of Maine's government. *Id. at § 16.* For an example of a Governor using the National Guard to help protect the Capitol, see *Me. Exec. Ord. 28 FY 20/21.*

VIII.
Legal Affairs

A. Role of Governor's Legal Counsel

1. **General.** Office legal counsel advise and represent the Governor in the Governor's official and not personal capacity. Such counsel also advises the Office as an organizational and governmental client. *Restatement of the Law (Third), The Law Governing Lawyers, § 96* (Representing Organization as a Client); and *id. at § 97* (Representing a Governmental Client). *Maine Rules of Professional Conduct, 1.11* (Special Conflicts-of-Interest of Former and Current Government Officers and Employees); *1.13* (Organization as Client).

2. **Professional Responsibilities.** Legal Counsel have duties of loyalty, competence, and diligence to represent the best interest of the client as defined by authorized persons exercising lawful business, managerial, and legal judgments. *Restatement Id. at § 96.* These duties attach even if the client's asserted rationale is of "doubtful utility or precedence." *Id. at § 97.*

   As with attorneys in all settings, these duties do not attach if the client's actions would violate law, constitute fraud, or constitute a crime. *Id.*; *M.R. Prof. C. 1.2(e).* These duties also do not attach if the client's actions would cause substantial public or private injury. *Id.* This is of particular note because the Governor and the office are impressed with a public trust to support and defend the state and federal constitutions, faithfully execute the laws, and otherwise faithfully discharge the duties of the office. *Art. IX, § 1;* and *Art. V, Pt. 1, § 12.*

3. **Advising Role.** Consistent with rules of professional responsibility, Governor's legal counsel:

   a. Should not be deterred from giving candid advice by the prospect that the advice will be unpalatable to the Governor. *ABA Model* and *Maine Rules of Professional Conduct 2.1, Comments 1.*

   b. May refer to relevant moral and ethical considerations in giving advice. Advice couched in narrow, purely legal terms may be of little value to a Governor, especially where practical considerations, such as cost or effects on other people, are predominant. *Id. at Comments 2 and 3.*

   c. Should recommend a course of action even when matters go beyond strictly legal questions, require the technical or policy expertise of another profession, and where experts provide conflicting advice. *Id. at Comments 4.*

   d. Should advise a Governor even if not asked to do so when counsel knows that a proposed course of action is likely to result in substantial adverse legal consequences to the Governor. *Id. at Comments 5.*

B. Privileges

1. **Attorney-Client Privilege.** "The lawyer-client privilege does not apply to communications between a public officer or agency and its lawyers. However, if the court

determines that disclosure will seriously impair the public officer's or agency's ability to process a claim or carry out a pending investigation, litigation, or proceeding in the public interest, the lawyer-client privilege will apply to communications concerning the pending investigation, claim, or action." *M. R. Evid. 502(d)(6).*

2. **Governmental Privilege.** "If the federal or Maine constitution, or a federal or Maine statute, creates a governmental privilege, a person may claim the privilege pursuant to the applicable provision of law. There is no other governmental privilege." *M. R. Evid. 508(a);* and *Restatement of the Law (Third), The Law Governing Lawyers § 74* (Privilege for a Governmental Client).

3. **Executive Privilege.** Generally speaking, executive privilege looks to protect from disclosure processes and work product that foster candid exploration, dissent, and early shaping of decisions. Despite the strong separation of powers provision in Art. III in the Maine Constitution, executive privilege does not appear to be a developed doctrine in Maine, perhaps because the Freedom of Access Act and its exceptions, *1 M.R.S. §§ 400 – 414*, largely govern such claims.

   Consequently, most executive law privilege is federal and, under those sources, an executive privilege is recognized only if the matter:

   a. directly affects the function of the executive at the highest level;

   b. does not relate to a charge of governmental misconduct;

   c. includes deliberative opinions and confidential recommendations, and not just facts; and

d. furthers the public and not a personal interest.

See, for example, 10 A.L.R. 4th at 355 (1981); Cox, Executive Privilege, 122 U. Pa. L. Rev. 1383 (1974); and *Hamilton v. Verdow, 414 A.2d 914, 921-26 (Md. 1980).*

C. Immunities and Liabilities

1. **From Injunctive Relief.** The Governor is immune from judicial coercion by mandamus or its procedural court order equivalent in performing official duties, whether those duties are ministerial or discretionary. *Kelly v. Curtis, 387 A.2d 426 (Me. 1972).* "The principle of separation and co-equality of powers is violated by the very process of the court's attempt to evaluate the nature of the official duty as ministerial or discretionary" and to coerce action based on that evaluation. *Id. at 429.* The Law Court has given the Governor a wide berth: "[F]or whatever [the Governor] does officially, the Governor shall answer only to his own conscience, to the people who elected him, and in case of the possible commission of a high crime or misdemeanor, to a court of impeachment." *Id. at 430.*

2. **From Money Damages.** As with all state employees, the Governor has certain immunity and/or limited liability for official and personal acts undertaken in good faith and in the course and scope of employment. *14 M.R.S. § 8101 et seq.*

   a. **Governmental Liability.** The Governor's protection from governmental liability includes, for example, not being liable for any claim that results from the following:

      (1) Undertaking or failing to adopt any order, rule, or policy, *id. at § 8104-B(1);*

(2) Undertaking or failing to grant, grant with conditions, refuse to grant or revoke any license, permit, order or other administrative approval or denial, *id. at § 8104-B(2);*

(3) Performing or failing to perform a discretionary function or duty, whether or not the discretion is abused and whether or not any statute, order, resolution, or policy under which the discretionary function or duty is performed is valid or invalid, *id. at § 8104-B(3);*

(4) Performing or failing to perform any prosecutorial function involving civil, criminal, or administrative enforcement, *id. at § 8104-B(4)*; and

(5) The activities of the state military force (of which as chief the Governor is part) when on duty, *id. at § 8104-B(5).*

b. Personal Liability. The Governor's protection from personal liability includes, for example, not being liable for the same claims noted above for governmental liability as well as:

(1) any intentional act or omission within the course and scope of employment; provided that the employee's actions are not found to have been in bad faith, *id. at § 8111(1)(E);* and

(2) any "discretionary act is reasonably encompassed by the duties of the governmental employee in question, regardless of whether the exercise of discretion is specifically authorized by statute, charter, ordinance, order, resolution, rule or resolve and shall be available to all governmental employees … who are required to exercise

judgment or discretion in performing their official duties." *Id. at § 8111(1)* and *(1)(C).*

c. **Eleventh Amendment Immunity.** The Governor cannot be sued in her official capacity in federal court without the state's consent. "The judicial power of the United States shall not … extend to any suit … commenced or prosecuted against one of the United States by citizens of another state." *U.S. Const. Amend. XI* (i.e., sovereign immunity). *See also Alden v. Maine, 527 U.S. 706 (1999);* and *The Federalist No. 45.*

D. Opinions of the Justices

The Governor has the authority to request an advisory opinion from the Justices of the Maine Supreme Judicial Court, *Art. VI, § 3* (and from the Attorney General under *5 M.R.S. § 195* discussed below*).*

1. **Solemn Occasion.** The Justices are obliged to answer only upon a "solemn occasion;" that is, when there is an important and specific question of law on an issue of live gravity (e.g., the taking of an official act relies upon the answer). *Opinion of the Justices, 123 A.3d 494 (2015).*

2. **Advisory, Non-Precedential.** Even then, the Justices' opinions are advisory only and not precedential. *See Maine Senate v. Secretary of State, 2018 ME 52.*

3. **Not a Proxy for Declaratory Relief.** Questions regarding the proper construction or constitutionality of an existing statute typically do not present a solemn occasion. *Opinion of the Justices, 355 A.2d 341, 390 (1976); Opinion of the Justices, 339 A.2d 483, 488-89 (1975).* Questions of whether a particular executive action under consideration would be "faithful" are better answered through a request for standard declaratory relief. *Opinion of the Justices, 147 Me. 410 (1952).*

E. Judicial Selection

1. **Nomination.** The Governor nominates judges of the district, superior and supreme courts. Probate judges are elected (except for vacancy appointments by the Governor), and family magistrates are appointed by the courts.

2. **ABA Standard.** In reviewing judicial candidates the rating standard used by the ABA for federal judges since 1953 is instructive: "well-qualified, qualified, or not qualified." *Process of the American Bar Association's Standing Committee on the Federal Judiciary.* Judicial nominees must have the integrity, professional competence, and judicial temperament fitting of a judge, and the law practice experience either in or otherwise suited to the particular demands of the court to which they are appointed. *Id.* For an elaboration of the qualifications, role, and appointment of judges, *see The Federalist Nos. 76-81* and *Langhauser, Nominations to the Supreme Court of the United States: Historical Lessons for Today's Debate, 205 Ed. L. Rep. 553 (2006).*

3. **Standard of Persuasion.** The standard of persuasion should be high. The Governor should be persuaded to a meaningful certainty that the individual has the character, temperament, discipline, and experience to serve capably.

4. **Advisory Committee.** Governors have a long tradition of using an advisory panel to review and make recommendations on judicial selection. *See, for example, Me. Exec. Ord. 7 FY 19/20.* Due diligence for new appointees includes confidential reviews from the bar, bench, and any disciplinary record held by bar counsel. Due diligence for re-appointees and elevations includes disclosure of any disciplinary record held by the Committee on Judicial Conduct.

5. **Application.** For an explanation of the application process and copies of the materials, see *https://www.maine.gov/Governor/mills/about/judicial_nominations.*

6. **Probate Judge Vacancies.** As regards the selection to fill a vacancy in a probate court judgeship:

    a. Vacancies may be caused by death, resignation, removal from the county, permanent incapacity, or any other reason. *4 M.R.S. § 301.*

    b. An appointee to fill a vacancy must be a Maine resident, a licensed Maine attorney, and enrolled in the same political party as the judge whose term is vacant. *Id.*

    c. In making the appointment, the Governor must choose from recommendations submitted by the county committee of the political party from which the appointment is to be made. *Id.* The Governor should also use a sub-committee of the Judicial Nominations Advisory Committee to review candidates.

    d. The appointee's term is the remainder of the predecessor's unexpired term. *Id.*

F. Inheriting Predecessor's Litigation

1. When new Governors take office, they commonly inherit their predecessor's ongoing official capacity litigation in state or federal courts.

2. State and federal rules of civil procedure provide that the new Governor is automatically substituted for the predecessor, *M.R. Civ. P. 25(d); Fed. R. Civ. P. 25(d).* This means that the new Governor must decide whether and if so how to proceed.

3. When the predecessor is a defendant, this means identifying possible and desired positions. When the predecessor is a plaintiff, this means possibly dismissing the complaint or appeal. When the predecessor is an amicus, this means possibly withdrawing from the case.

4. For an example of a new Governor substituting and obtaining dismissal as a plaintiff from her predecessor's action, see *Texas v. United States, No. 1:18-cv-00068 (S.D. Tex. Jan. 25, 2019)* (no longer seeking to strike down claim regarding the Deferred Action for Childhood Arrivals (DACA) program).

G. Managing Social Media Accounts

1. The interactive space of a Governor's social media account (such as Twitter and Facebook) may qualify as a designated public forum. If so, access to the site and content of the speech may be subject to constitutional protection. This means that speakers may have a right to be heard and other users may have a right to hear what those speakers may have to say on those sites. If so, deleting posts or blocking posters because of their viewpoints may constitute viewpoint discrimination.

2. As general rules of thumb, clearly "official" sites will implicate these rules, and exclusively personal sites will not. Sites denominated as "personal" but open for expressive activity by the public, and the Governor uses the account in part to speak about issues falling within the Governor's official duties, will be the more difficult case. There, as with all First Amendment cases, determinations will be very fact reliant.

3. Two examples to consider:

   a. First, *see Leuthy v. LePage, No. cv-1:17-00296 (D. Me. 2018).* This case involved a Facebook campaign account continued as Governor that deleted posts and blocked users based on the content of the viewpoints. The complaint settled with a publicly available agreement that is informative.

   b. Second, *see Knight First Amendment Institute v. Trump, 928 F.3d 226 (2nd Cir. 2018).* This case involved a President's official Twitter account that blocked users based on the viewpoint of their posts. The federal district and appellate courts ruled for the plaintiffs and the case was dismissed on cert as moot because the President had been expelled by Twitter from the platform. *Biden v. Knight First Amendment Institute, 593 U.S. _ (2021).* Nonetheless, the Second Circuit's opinion cited above remains informative.

H. Deeds Conveying DOT Surplus Property. The Governor, on recommendation of the Department of Transportation, may sell and convey on behalf of the state the interests of the state in property taken or acquired by purchase for transportation purposes and deemed no longer necessary for those purposes. *23 M.R.S. § 61(2).* This occurs with some regularity.

I. Commercial Use of the State Seal. Commercial use of the State seal is subject to the Governor's approval. *1 M.R.S. § 204.*

IX.
Relationship to the Attorney General

A. Legislative Election. Unlike the Governor who is elected by the people, the Attorney General is elected by the Legislature. *Art. IX, § 11.* Maine is the only state that selects its Attorney General in this manner. In 43 states, the Attorney General is elected. In five states, the Governor appoints, and in one state the state supreme court appoints.

B. Common Law Powers. The Attorney General is an office without powers specified by the Constitution. The powers of the office derive from common law, and the Attorney General is endowed with all common law powers not otherwise restricted by statute or the constitution. *Lund ex rel. Wilbur v. Pratt, 308 A.2d 554, 558 (Me. 1973); Superintendent of Insurance v. Attorney General, 558 A.2d 1197 (Me. 1989); State v. Fisheries, 120 Me. 121 (1921).* These powers include the authority to join litigation without direction or consent of the Governor or the Legislature. *LePage v. Mills,* CV-17-185 *(Me. Super. Ct., Oct. 12, 2018).*

C. Advisory Opinions

1. The Governor can request a written opinion on a question of law from the Attorney General. *5 M.R.S. § 195.*

Such opinions are advisory and are not binding upon the Governor. Again, a complete set of these opinions can be found at *https://www.maine.gov/legis/lawlib/lldl/agops/agmaster.html,* best searched using the search feature of an internet browser (as opposed to a search feature of the webpage itself).

2. In recent times (since 1991), the attorneys general have trended to issue fewer written advisory opinions to the executive and Legislature, and to instead provide advisory opinions orally. This may relate in part to the fact that all six attorneys general who served since then have themselves been former legislators and are therefore more comfortable communicating with each branch in that less formal manner.

3. A gold standard for Maine A.G. opinions are those signed by Assistant, and then Deputy, Attorney General Stephen L. Diamond between 1976 and 1982. Clear, tight, and always devoid of extraneous influences.

D. Serving As Counsel for the Governor. The Attorney General has the authority and duty to provide both general legal services to and represent the Governor and executive branch agencies.

1. **Legal Services Generally.** "All legal services required by those officers, boards and commissions in matters relating to their official duties" must be rendered by or at the direction of the Attorney General. *5 M.R.S. § 191(3).*

2. **Litigation**

   a. The Attorney General "shall appear for the State, the head of any state department, the head of any state institution and agencies of the State in all civil actions and proceedings in which the State is a party or interested, or when requested by the Governor or by the Legislature or either House of the Legislature." *Id. at § 191.*

b. All such actions and proceedings must be prosecuted or defended by or at the direction of the Attorney General. *Id.*

c. As discussed further below, although this statute expressly refers to a Governor's or Legislature's request for certain representation, the Attorney General's authority to appear are broader than any such request. *LePage v. Mills, No. CV-17-185 (Me. Super. Ct. Oct. 12, 2018).* The Attorney General may "institute, conduct, and maintain all such actions and proceedings as [s]he deems necessary for the enforcement of the laws of the State, the preservation of order, and the protection of public rights" even if not so requested. *Id. at 4-6.*

When there is no disagreement on law or policy such that the Governor and Attorney General are aligned, the operation of *5 M.R.S. § 191* is straightforward. Indeed, in most instances, the offices of Governor and Attorney General work well together. This was certainly true during the pandemic when there was close cooperation on the executive orders and litigation defenses. *See, for example, the cases, cited Chapter VI B.7(a) and (b).*

E. **Authorizing the Governor to Have Other Counsel.** When the Governor and Attorney General disagree and are not so aligned, the Attorney General must decide whether to represent the Governor or authorize other counsel.

1. **Approval Required.** The Governor may not "employ private counsel except upon prior written approval of the

Attorney General." *Id. at § 191(3).* Such approval by the Attorney General is discretionary.

2. **Control and Payment.** If the Attorney General authorizes the Governor to have outside counsel, the:

   a. Attorney General may not exercise the approval authority in a manner that controls the representation, *Opinion of the Justices, 2015 ME 27;* and

   b. Governor cannot compel the Attorney General to pay for such counsel from the Attorney General's budget. *LePage v. Mills, CV-17-95 (Me. Super. Ct., Oct. 16, 2017).*

3. **Factors Influencing the Decision.** The decision to authorize other counsel is not simply one of conflict of interest under the bar rules. *Superintendent of Insurance v. Attorney General, 558 A.2d 1197 (1989).* As the Law Court has explained:

> Because of the multiple duties imposed on the office, the status of the Attorney General is unique. As a member of the bar, he is subject to the ethical standards of the bar, but he is also a constitutional officer charged with common law and statutory duties and powers. As an officer of government he is directed to control and manage the litigation of the State by providing counsel to state agencies and by approving the retention of private counsel. Of at least equal importance, however, is his role as the legal representative of the people of the State in pursuing the public interest. *Id. at 1202.*

The Attorney General has "wide" and "considerable discretion and autonomy" in determining whether the "public interest" is served by not representing the Governor and, further yet, by taking a position opposing the Governor. *Id. at 1199—1200.*

F. Litigation Scenarios When Governor and Attorney General Are Not Aligned. There are a variety of ways in which the Governor and Attorney General may oppose one another in litigation.

1. **Amicus Briefs.** Governors often want to sign on to a National (NGA), Democratic (DGA), or Republican (RGA) Governors' Associations or others' briefs in litigation outside of Maine. Likewise, Attorney Generals often seek to do the same with the National (NAAG), Democratic (DAAG), or Republican (RAAG) Attorneys General Associations or others' briefs.

   In these amicus cases, the Governor and Attorney General should advise one another in advance. The Attorney General does not need the Governor's consent to join, for example, a NAAG brief. And the Attorney General should permit the Governor to join "as Governor" an NGA brief, even if the Attorney General asserts in that case a different position on "behalf of the State."

   These are typically not contentious unless the case involves a consequential issue, and the outcome may have a consequential effect for Maine. Sometimes, the opposition can be direct and formal. *See, for example, California v. Texas, 141 S. Ct. 2104 (2021)* where the Governor and Attorney General were taking opposing positions on the constitutionality of the Affordable Care Act. Other times, the opposition can be more informal. *See, for example, Quill v. North Dakota, 504 U.S. 298 (1992),* which engendered an unusual procedural posture.

   In *Quill*, Maine's Governor joined as "Governor of the State of Maine" an amicus brief submitted by the attorneys general from two states supporting a position to protect L.L. Bean from having to collect North Dakota sales tax on out-of-state catalogue sales. The Maine Attorney General agreed with the opposing view of attorneys general from 16 other states but did not join their brief. Instead, the Maine Attorney General wrote to the Clerk of the Supreme Court to say that the Maine Governor's amicus position did not represent "the State of Maine." The Clerk replied that any such questions about that distinction, while perhaps a matter of concern in Maine, was not a matter of concern for the Court.

Since then, the Court has expressly said in a related context that "respect for state sovereignty must … take into account the authority of a State to structure its executive branch in a way that empowers multiple officials to defend its sovereign interests in federal court." *Cameron v. EMW Women's Surgical Center, 595 U.S. __ (2022), quoting from Virginia House of Delegates v. Bethune-Hill, 139 S.Ct. 1945 (2019).* This recognition suggests that federal courts are likely to be lenient in hearing separately from a state Attorney General and Governor as amici regardless of any turf war back home.

2. **Requests for Opinions of the Justices.** When requesting an opinion of the justices on an important question of law under *Art. VI, § 3,* the Governor may submit a memorandum in support of a particular position. Thereafter the Attorney General may ask the justices to entertain the Attorney General's competing or opposing view. As a matter of comity the justices typically consider both positions.

There are several good examples of this dynamic. *E.g., Opinion of the Justices, 578 A.2d 183 (Me. 1990)* (upholding the state election law's minimum vote requirement); *Opinion of the Justices, 571 A.2d 1169 (Me. 1989)* (upholding Governor's right to receive bond enactors under state Presentment Clause); and *Opinion of the Justices, 571*

A.2d 805 (Me. 1989) (upholding Governor's duty not to sign an enactor that violated federal Supremacy Clause).

3. **Governor as a Defendant with Private Counsel and Attorney General Not in the Litigation.** Sometimes, the Attorney General lets the Governor answer a private party with the Governor's own lawyer and the Attorney General sits it out. *See, for example, Coastal Counties Workforce Inc. v. LePage, No. 1:17-cv-00417 (D. Me. 2018)* (Governor cannot withhold $8 million in federal job training funds from three regional workforce boards).

4. **Attorney General Intervenes to Sue the Governor.** Sometimes, the Attorney General determines that the public interest requires the Attorney General to intervene in opposition to the Governor. *See, for example, Washington County Commissioners v. Commissioner of DOC, AP-18-06 (Mar. 14, 2018)* (declaring unlawful Governor's prison closure in face of facility recognition language and then current funding); and *Mayhew v. Burwell, No. 14–1300 (1st Cir. Nov. 2014)* (cert. denied) (Medicaid coverage dispute).

5. **Governor Sues the Attorney General.** Sometimes, the Governor decides to sue the Attorney General. *See, for example, LePage v. Mills, CV-17-185 (Me. Super. Ct., Oct.12, 2018)* (Governor seeking to block Attorney General from appearing in an out-of-state action); *LePage v. Mills, CV-17-216 (Me. Super. Ct., Oct. 1, 2018)* (Governor seeking to compel FOAA disclosure of Attorney General's work product documents); and *LePage v. Mills, CV-17-95 (Me. Super. Ct., Oct. 16, 2017)* (Governor seeking to compel Attorney General to pay for the Governor's outside counsel).

6. **Governor Intervenes to Oppose the Attorney General.** Finally, there has been one unusual case where the Governor intervened to defend the constitutionality of a law when the Attorney General refused to do so. *Gallagher v. McKernan, No. cv-90-0256-B (D. Me. 1990)* (transcript of oral ruling on Oct. 26, 1990, in *Appendix*; no written and reported opinion). This case is of note because defending statutes is a core responsibility of the Attorney General.

   Preceding this case, in *Opinion of the Justices, 578 A.2d 183 (Me. 1990)*, the Justices found for the Governor and against the Attorney General on the constitutionality of an election statute. Ten weeks later, a private party in *Gallagher* sued the Governor and Secretary of State in federal court on essentially the same question.

   Despite the Justices' prior opinion that the election statute was constitutional, and noting that any statute is presumed to be constitutional, the Attorney General sought to concede. He declined to represent the Governor in *Gallagher*; agreed to represent the Secretary; would not defend the Justices' opinion; and joined a motion to dismiss the Governor.

   The federal court found that the Governor's constitutionally required role in the lawmaking process gave him standing to present a defense for the statute. Accordingly, the court granted the Governor's motion for permissive intervention under *Fed. R. Civ. P. 24(b)*. The court then ruled for the Governor on the merits; upheld the statute; and issued an uncommon lecture to the Attorneys General about their positions in the case. *Id.* (transcript of oral ruling in *Appendix*).

7. **Judicial Resolution of These Disputes.** Several of the above disputes were marked in part by partisanship or ambition more than earnest legal debates. The courts, however, have routinely upheld positions based on legal analysis regardless of office. For example:

a. Between 1989 and 1991, the Governor was 4-0 against the Attorney General. *See* the four cases cited in *subsections F(2) and (6) above.*

b. Yet between 2014 and 2018, the Attorney General was at least 6-0 against the Governor in litigation on material issues. *See* the six cases cited in *subsections F(3), (4) and (5) above,* as well as *Maine Municipal Association v. Mahew, 1:14-cv-00311 (D. Me. Dec. 2014)* (General Assistance dispute).

These ten cases consistently show the courts eschewing motives of partisanship and personal ambition for legal reasoning. But one opinion was viewed by some as possibly pandering to politics when it used 55 pages to reject a Governor's challenge in a seemingly straight-forward presentment case. *Opinion of the Justices, 2015 ME 107* (Governor missed the 10-day window to sign or return 65 bills so they all became law without signature).

G. **A Broader View of the Tensions.** Other states, despite their differing manners of electing or selecting the Attorney General, also wrestle with questions about the reach of each officer's powers. *See, for example, Hartley v. Clausen, 264 P. 403 (Wash. 1928).* When the relations are strained in Maine, there can be several reasons or accelerants.

1. **Reasonable Disagreements on the Law.** Finally there is, of course, often room for reasonable disagreements on how a law may be best interpreted and thus most faithfully executed. These debates become more consequential when the questions regard the scope of power or duty, or high-profile social or fiscal issues.

2. **Misunderstanding "Supreme" Executive Power.** Ambitious Governors may read *Art. III, § 1* to say that there are only three branches of government; the Attorney General's law enforcement role is executive in character; and the Governor has the "supreme executive power" under *Art. V, Pt. 1, § 1.* But this view ignores, as discussed above the independent nature of the Attorney General's common law powers. *Superintendent of Insurance v. Attorney General, 558 A.2d 1197 (Me. 1989).*

3. **Legislative Expectations and Job Security.** Because the Legislature elects and possibly re-elects the Attorney General, legislators often see the Attorney General as "their" lawyer and they often expect the Attorney General to align with their priorities. This creates its own tension for any Attorney General, and it can accelerate when the Legislature and Governor are on opposing sides of the matter at issue, or when the deputy Attorney General is seeking to become Attorney General.

4. **Political Partisanship.** When the Legislature and Governorship are controlled by different parties, and further yet when the Legislature and Attorney General are in the same party in opposition to the Governor, there is more opportunity for partisan policy disagreements.

5. **Personal Ambition.** Nationally, an office of Attorney General is often a steppingstone to the office of Governor. Since 1970, Maine has had eleven attorneys general and five have run for Governor (two successfully). When an Attorney General seeks to become Governor, or is a former political rival of a Governor, there is again more opportunity for partisan differences.

H. Like Tension at the Federal Level. At the federal level, there is like tension between the Department of Justice Office of Legal Counsel (OLC) and the White House Counsel (WHC). This is because the distinct roles of OLC and WHC can yield different approaches and thus different positions.

1. On the one hand, the OLC consists of lawyers without executive responsibilities and limited policy expertise. They pursue a "best view of the law," which is essentially a legal-only four-corners analysis consciously intended to be independent and insulated from political and policy pressures. OLC argues that this "best view" approach produces the most faithful interpretation and therefore the most faithful execution. *U.S. D.O.J. OLC Memorandum re: Best Practices for OLC Legal Advice and Written Opinions (July 16, 2012) (updating Memorandum of May 16, 2005).*

2. The WHC, on the other hand, consists of lawyers with executive responsibilities and access to significant policy expertise. These responsibilities and expertise urge the WHC to start with the four-corners analysis but then consider policy implications to test whether there is more than one viable option for the executive to consider. By this approach, the executive can choose which interpretation best meets the facts and important policy objectives implicated by those facts. For this reason, the WHC argues that this approach produces the most faithful interpretation and execution. *See, for example, Bauer, The National Security Lawyer in Crisis: When the Best View of the Law May Not be the Best View, NYU School of Law, Working Research Paper No. 17-08 (2017)* (discussing national security) (hereinafter Bauer).

3. Again, the OLC and WHC have distinct roles that produce different points of emphasis. For OLC, "too much" policy infusion unduly strains faithful interpretation and therefore faithful execution. For WHC, "not enough"

policy infusion abdicates the duty to ensure that the decision-making lawfully maximizes the opportunity to address meaningfully the problem at hand.

4. But the underlying question here appears to be whether faithful execution necessarily accommodates a single "best view" or, alternatively, whether it can accommodate several rationally based and therefore lawfully faithful views. The answer is better found as-applied than in the abstract, which is why those two offices—like our state offices—must talk, push, pull, and attempt to reconcile on the given issues of the day.

5. For more on the WHC view, see Bauer at *id.* For a criticism of Bauer, see *DeRosa, National Security Lawyering: The Best View of the Law as a Regulative Ideal, 31 Geo. J. Legal Ethics 277 (2018).* For more on the OLC view, see *Moss, Executive Branch Legal Interpretation: A Perspective From The Office Of Legal Counsel, 52 Admin. L. Rev. 1303 (2000).* For broader discussions of executive branch constitutional interpretation, see articles cited in *Johnsen, Guidelines for the President's Legal Advisors, 81 Ind. L. J. 1345, fn. 4 (2006).*

6. Note that the American Bar Association's Model Rules of Professional Conduct, and the analogous Maine Rule, takes account of the WHC view.

    a. "In representing a client, a lawyer shall exercise independent professional judgment and render candid advice. In rendering advice, a lawyer may refer not only to law but to other considerations such as moral, economic, social, and political factors, that may be relevant to the client's situation. "*ABA Model Rule 2.1* and *Maine Rule of Professional Conduct 2.1.*

b. "Although a lawyer is not a moral advisor as such, moral and ethical considerations impinge upon most legal questions and may decisively influence how the law will be applied." *Id. at Rules 2.1* and *Comments 2.*

I. The Best Way Forward? In any pluralist society, there must be sound ways for the government to balance its competitive interests and to legitimize its critical decisions. *Langhauser, Nominations to the Supreme Court of the United States: Historical Lessons for Today's Debate, 205 Educ. L. Rep. 553 (2006), citing Murphy, Elements Of Judicial Strategy 17 (1964).* As with bicameralism and separation of powers, reconciliation of the chief executive and law enforcement officers' roles requires sophistication, good faith, respect, and moderation. As observed by one who has held both offices when relations were both trying and sound:

> Keep the channels of communication open and keep the wheels of government turning. The public expects its officials to trust one another and to maintain a day-to-day working relationship. *Mills, NAAG Fall Conference (Dec. 1, 2015).*

X.
Clemency and Extraditions

A. **Clemency**: Pardons and Commutations

1. **Nature.** The Governor has the powers to pardon criminal convictions and commute sentences of imprisonment. *Art. V, Pt. 1, § 11.* A pardon is an official forgiveness of a crime; pardons are not used for civil offenses or administrative judgements. A pardon does not expunge a record; it only adds to the record. A commutation releases a person from a sentence, typically from confinement. The Governor also has the powers to "remit after conviction all forfeitures and penalties, and to grant reprieves," *id.*, although there is little evidence of use of this provision to return funds or items previously seized to persons whose sentence was commuted.

2. **Regulations.** Clemency powers are subject to "regulations relative to the manner of applying" for such clemency. *15 M.R.S. §§ 2161-2167.* But neither legislative, judicial, nor administrative action on sentencing can infringe upon and thereby usurp either the pardon or commutation power. For such commutation cases, see *Bossie v. State, 488 A.2d 477 (Me. 1985)* and *Baston v. Robbins, 153 Me. 128 (1957)* (Legislature); *State v. Hunter, 447 Me. 797 (1982)* (Legislature and courts); *State v. Sturgis, 110 Me.*

96 (1912) (courts); and *Austin v. State, 663 A.2d 62 (Me. 1995) (*parole board*).*

3. **Petition Process.** For details of the process as well as the petition used, see *https://www.maine.gov/corrections/sites/maine.gov.corrections/files/inline-files/2019%20pardon%20application.pdf.*

4. **Practice and Policy.** As a matter of traditional policy and practice, pardons and commutations:

   a. Are rare, with commutations being even rarer. The standard of proof should be high. The Governor should be persuaded to a meaningful certainty that the individual is of the maturity, character, and discipline to behave well under a grant so that the decision will reflect well on both the individual and the Governor.

   b. Are intended to recognize exceptionally good behavior since conviction. They are not intended to rectify wrongful charges, convictions, or sentences, which is the intended province of the criminal justice process.

   c. They are typically not given for violent, sexual, abusive, OUI, or other egregious or dangerous offenses. They are also typically not given in order to restore a person's right to possess a firearm revoked by force of *15 M.R.S. § 393* (prohibiting certain person form possessing a firearm upon certain convictions).

   d. The Governor's powers of pardon do not reach those who have been impeached. *Art. V, Pt. 1, § 11.*

5. **Advisory Committee.** Governors have a long tradition of using an advisory panel to review and make recommendations on petitions for a pardon or for clemency. *See, for*

example, Me. Exec. Ord. 6 FY 19/20. Such a panel determines which petitions receive hearings and recommends to the Governor its judgment on each such petition.

6. **Copies of Warrants.** Pardons and commutations that are granted are issued on a warrant, and copies thereof are filed with the arresting police department, prosecuting office, clerk of pertinent court, State Bureau of Identification, Attorney General's office, and Secretary of State. *See, for example, 15 M.R.S. § 2166.*

7. **Other Sources.** For a thoughtful elaboration of the clemency power generally, see *The Federalist No. 74.* For a helpful analogue to the federal clemency powers, see the U.S. D.O.J. Office of the Pardon Attorney at *https://www.justice.gov/pardon.*

B. Extraditions

1. **Nature.** Extraditions move prisoners from one state to another. The Governor may request that a prisoner held in another state be sent to Maine to face charges for a crime committed here or be asked to send a prisoner held in Maine to another state to face charges for a crime committed there.

2. **State Statutes and Federal Origin.** Extraditions proceed in the manner provided by the Uniform Criminal Extradition Act, *15 M.R.S. § 201 et seq.,* and the Interstate Compact on Detainers, *34-A M.R.S. § 9601 et seq.* Court procedure governing extradition from Maine is set by *M.R.U. Crim. P. 85 – 87.* The origin of extradition power is, however, federal. It flows from the Full Faith and Credit Clause of the U.S. Constitution which provides that "full faith and credit shall be given in each state to the public acts, records, and judicial proceedings of every other state." *U.S. Const. Art. IV, § 1.*

3. **Paperwork.** Extradition paperwork is prepared by the criminal division of the Attorney General's office for the Governor to review and execute.

4. **Litigation Precedent.** For one case of note on this subject, see the Law Court's refusal to enjoin a Maine Governor from extraditing a prisoner to face a death penalty in another state, *Joubert v. McKernan, 588 A.2d 748 (1991).*

C. Other Related

1. **Uniform Interstate Family Support Act.** The Governor may demand that the Governor of another state surrender an individual found in the other state who is charged criminally in Maine with having failed to provide for the support of an obliged person; and upon demand by the Governor of another state, surrender an individual found in Maine who is charged criminally in the other state with having failed to provide for required support. *19-A M.R.S. § 3351(2).*

2. **Interpleader Compact.** The Interpleader Compact is an interstate compact among Maine, New Hampshire, New Jersey, New York, and Pennsylvania. It gives courts the power to obtain jurisdiction over property in the member states relating to a number of claims against stakeholders. Stakeholders can include banks and insurance agencies, among others. The Governor oversees this Compact. *14 M.R.S. § 6403.*

XI.
Executive Orders and Proclamations

A. Executive Orders

1. **Defined.** An executive order is a means to command focused attention or action through a reasonable interpretation of an existing law. Orders that purport to apply broad-based rules without such a basis may be challenged as being lawmaking in character and therefore a usurpation of legislative power in violation of separation of powers. To withstand such challenge, orders should carefully cite the law(s) that they are executing. One good such example is *Me. Exec. Ord. 57 FY 19/20.*

2. **Copies.** Governors typically post copies of their executive orders and proclamations on their office websites. A copy of each executive order must be filed with the Legislative Council and the Law and Legislative Reference Library within one week of issuance. *1 M.R.S. § 521.*

3. **Duration.** Orders of previous Governors may be revoked but they remain in effect—even if not in practice enforced—until so revoked.

4. **Examples.** The style, form, sourcing, detail, tone, and reach of executive orders has varied widely over time. To see how Governors have exercised various powers and duties

by executive order, a comprehensive collection is available at *https://Legislature.maine.gov/legis/lawlib/lldl/execorders/eomaster.html.* They may be best searched by subject using the search feature of an internet browser (as opposed to a search feature of the webpage itself).

B. Proclamations

1. **Introduction.** Various statutes require or authorize the Governor to issue a proclamation or, less formally, a declaration. A declaration is a formal finding of fact that is set forth in any written manner but not on the formal "proclamation" stationary. In some instances, the statutes require the Governor to issue a proclamation as a ceremonial act to commemorate an event or certain persons. In other instances, statutes require a proclamation as a form of certification or announcement to trigger the beginning of other acts. In the most important instances, though, the statutes authorize a Governor to issue a proclamation when, in the Governor's discretion, a current urgency to act exists, and additional powers need to be invoked in order to meet the needs presented by that urgency.

2. **Ceremonial Proclamations.** Ceremonial proclamations are only instruments of communication; they do not define legal rights and do not assign legal duties; and, therefore, do not act with the force of law. Some ceremonial proclamations may be inadvisable because their content (such as proclaiming "Bible Week" given the Establishment Clause) may raise questions about propriety. For leading examples of ceremonial proclamations, such as Wyeth Day, see *1 M.R.S. §§ 111-A-150-Q* and *17 M.R.S. § 1315.*

3. **Proclamations That Certify Results or Initiate Actions.** This category consists primarily of the following.

   a. **Elections.** *See Chapter XIV, Administering Elections.*

   b. **Other.** For example, submitting municipal charter changes to voters (*30-A M.R.S. § 1324*); constitutional amendment adoption (*1 M.R.S. § 352*); and social security contingency action (*26 M.R.S. § 1050*).

4. **Proclamations That Invoke Powers**. This category consists primarily of the following categories:

   a. **General**

      (1) Civil emergencies as broadly referenced in *37-B M.R.S. §§ 741-742* and disasters specifically defined in *id. at* § *703(2).*

   b. **Other Public Health**

      (1) Extreme public health emergency, *22 M.R.S. § 802(2-A)* (declaration); and

      (2) Radiation hazards, *25 M.R.S. § 50.*

   c. **Other Public Safety**

      (1) Use of state police reserve corps, *id. at § 1505*;

      (2) Insurrection, *37-B M.R.S. § 182*; and

      (3) Emergency location of state government, *1 M.R.S. § 711.*

   d. **Natural Resources**

      (1) Forest fires, *12 M.R.S. § 9001*;

      (2) Oil spills, *38 M.R.S. § 547* and *37-B M.R.S. § 742(3);* and

(3) Hunting closures, *12 M.R.S. § 10105(15).*

e. **Economic Conditions**

(1) Banking emergency, *9-B M.R.S. § 151*;

(2) Insurance emergency, *24-A M.R.S. § 471*;

(3) Abnormal market disruption, *10 M.R.S. § 1105* (declaration); and

(4) Energy related emergency, *37-B M.R.S. § 742(2).*

5. **Attestation.** Proclamations that are not ceremonial are attested to by the Secretary of State who also affixes a State Seal thereto and receives an original copy thereof. *See, for example, id. at § 742(1)(A).*

6. **Copies.** The Maine State Archives maintains a complete paper file of proclamations. There is no comprehensive online collection of proclamations, but the Archives has digitized some of them at *https://digitalmaine.com/arc_executive_proclamations/* (more recent proclamations) and *https://archives.maine.gov/objects?limit=digital_object* (older).

XII.
Flag Protocol

A. **Background.** Lowering flags to half-staff on the occasion of a death is a subject requiring regular attention. The issues here are informed by state and federal law and traditional protocols.

B. **Jurisdiction.** The laws apply only to public or government buildings. Private citizens may make their own decisions about the flags on their own property.

C. **Federal Law.** Federal law speaks only to the United States flag although state flags as a practical matter typically follow suit. Federal law requires both the President and Governors to lower the U.S. flag to half-staff for the death of specified federal officials and authorizes the President to lower the U.S. flag upon the death of certain other federal or foreign officials. *4 U.S.C. § 7(m).* Federal law also authorizes the Governor to lower the U.S. flag upon the death of numerous other specified officials. For that list of officials, *see id.* and *34 U.S.C. §10284.*

D. **State Law.** Maine has adopted the national Uniform Flag Law which speaks to both the U.S. and Maine flags, and to the authorities of both the President and the Governor. For those details, see *1 M.R.S. §§ 251-256.*

E. **Protocols and Traditional Practices.** Law Library research shows that Governors between 1998 to 2019 used their discretion to lower flags as follows.

1. **Diverse Instances.** Recent Governors have used their discretion to lower flags for deaths involving a severe national tragedy, firefighters in another state, local servicemen, older decorated veterans, local police, and fire fighters killed in the line of duty, current and former legislators, county commissioners, city councilors, tribal leaders, civic leaders, business leaders, and even a "tireless organic farming advocate."

2. **Timing and Location(s).** To provide clarity and consistency across the state, a Governor's statements need to indicate when the lowering starts, when it ends, and where it occurs.

   a. **Timing.** Governors most often lowered flags during the daylight hours of the day of the service. For very prominent persons, the flags were lowered from the day of death until the end of the day of the service. When the date of such a service is unknown (because of weather, religion, or other), Governors issued ensuing statements with that updated information.

   b. **Location(s).** For national and statewide figures, Governors typically order flags lowered across the state. For more regional or county figures, the order is typically across the affected region or county. For more local figures, the order is typically for a municipality or municipalities or, even more narrowly, for certain building(s) (like a town hall, school, or fire department) within a municipality.

3. **Other.** Regardless of whether a flag is flown at full- or half-staff, flags are only to be flown between the hours of sunrise and sunset unless the flag is properly illuminated during the hours of darkness. *4 U.S.C. § 6(a).*

XIII.
Appointment and Management of Personnel

A. Appointments

1. **Generally.** The Governor's appointments include:

   a. the heads of departments and members of boards and commissions, *5 M.R.S. § 931(1)(C);*

   b. all "judicial officers" except judges of probate and justices of the peace, *Art. V, Pt. 1, § 8;*

   c. dedimus justices, *5 M.R.S. §* 4;

   d. extraterritorial commissioners of deeds, *33 M.R.S. § 251;*

   e. public administrators, *18-C M.R.S. § 3-619*; and

   f. any civil and military officer whose appointment is not otherwise provided for by the constitution or statute. *Art. V, Pt. 1, § 8.*

2. **Reappointment.** The power to appoint includes the power to reappoint. *Longley v. State Employees Appeals Board, 392 A.2d 529 (Me. 1978).*

3. **Notice.** "Every nomination by the Governor shall be made 7 days at least prior to appointment of the nominee." *Art. V, Pt. 1, § 8.*

4. **Direct Appointments.** For appointments not requiring confirmation, the appointees have 30 days to take their oath and 45 days to file with the Secretary of State. *5 M.R.S. § 6.* These and prospective appointees may begin serving once they take their oaths.

5. **Confirmed Appointments.** For appointees requiring legislative confirmation, the hearing must be held within 30 (35 for judges) days of the posting date; and the committee vote must be held within 35 (40 for judges) days of posting. *3 M.R.S. § 157.* The senate vote must then be held within 45 (50 for judges) days of posting. *3 M.R.S. § 158.* Nominations not meeting these timeframes expire and must be reposted and the nominating process restarted. With few exceptions (such as Ethics Commission appointees who have only 10 days, *1 M.R.S. § 1002(3),* confirmed appointees have 30 days following their confirmation vote to take their oath and 45 days from such vote to file their certificate of qualification with the Secretary of State. *5 M.R.S. § 6.* They may begin serving once they take their oaths.

6. **Prospective Appointments.** The general rule is that executive power of appointment may not be exercised unless and until a vacancy in office exists, but the Governor may make a "prospective appointment" by posting a nominee and setting a specific start date when the seat will be vacant, provided such future date is during the Governor's term. *Op. Me. Atty. Gen. (June 9, 1976); Pattangall v. Gilman, 115 Me. 344 (1916).*

7. **Administering Oaths.** The Governor administers oaths to all judges of the Supreme, Superior, and District Courts, "and all state officials elected by the Legislature." *5 M.R.S.*

§ 5. "Every other person elected or appointed to any civil office shall take and subscribe the oath before any dedimus justice commissioned by the Governor for that purpose, except when the Constitution otherwise provides." *Id.*

8. **Signing Commissions.** All commissions for appointees must be signed by the Governor, attested by the secretary or a deputy of the secretary, and have the seal of the state affixed thereto. *Art. IX § 3.*

9. **Tenure.** Appointees serve for four-year terms, *5 M.R.S. § 2,* or during the pleasure of the Governor unless otherwise provided by law. *Art. IX, § 6.* Specific terms are often set by law. For example, a term may be set in the constitution (judges for 7-year terms with a six-month holdover extension in *Art. VI, § 4),* a public law (Maine Community College System trustees for four-year terms in *20-A M.R.S. § 12705(2),* or a private and special law (Maritime Academy trustees for five-year terms in *P. & S.L. 1967, ch. 177).*

   An appointee may serve until a successor fills the position, even if that period is beyond their appointed term. *5 M.R.S. § 3.* But there are certain positions where the constitution or statutes fix the length of an appointee's holdover. *See, for example,* judges at *Art. VI, § 4* (six-month extension limit), the Board of Environmental Protection at *38 M.R.S. § 341-C(3)* (one year extension limit), and the Land Use Planning Commission at *12 M.R.S. § 683-A(4)* (extension limited to the time "required to ensure fair consideration of specific major applications pending before the commission").

10. **Filling Certain Vacancies by Appointment.** The Governor may fill the following positions if they become vacant:

    a. United States Senator, *U.S. Const. Art. I, § 3, ¶ 2* and *21-A M.R.S. § 391(1)* (proclaiming special election);

b. United States Representative, *U.S. Const. Art. I, § 2, ¶ 4* and *21-A M.R.S. § 392* (proclaiming special election);

c. State Attorney General, *Art. IX, § 11* (with the approval of the Judiciary Committee and confirmation by the Senate)*;*

d. County Sheriffs, *Art. IX, § 10* and *30-A M.R.S. § 441;*

e. Judges of the Supreme, Superior, and District Courts (with the approval of the Judiciary Committee and confirmation by the Senate), *Art. V, Pt. 1, § 8;*

f. The "appointive or elective head of any agency, board, commission or department" (such as a commissioner) when there is no state employee "duly authorized by law to exercise the powers and perform the duties" of such head during the vacancy. *5 M.R.S. § 1*;

g. District attorney, *30-A M.R.S. § 252(2);*

h. County Probate Judges, *Art. VI, § 6*. For the unique details of this particular process, see *Chapter VII, Legal Affairs*;

i. Chief medical examiner, *22 M.R.S. § 3022 (1);*

j. County Treasurers, *30-A M.R.S. § 151(3);*

k. County Commissioners, *30-A M.R.S. 63(3);* and

l. Registers of Probate, *18-C M.R.S. § 1-501(3).*

11. Appointing Sitting Legislators. The Governor cannot appoint sitting legislators to executive or judicial positions. *See Chapter IV(B)(9).*

12. **Prohibition on Interbranch Appointments.** The Constitution expressly provides that "the powers of this government shall be divided into 3 distinct departments, the legislative, executive and judicial," and that "no person or persons, belonging to one of these departments, shall exercise any of the powers properly belonging to either of the others, except in the cases herein expressly directed or permitted." *Me. Const. Art. III, §§ 1 and 2.* To enforce this separation, *5 M.R.S. § 12012* limits, subject to exceptions such as the advisory nature the board, the authority to appoint, for example, a legislator to an executive branch board. But note that this statute is so poorly drafted that its precise meaning is not clear and it has not been formally interpreted.

B. Management

1. **Supervision.** The Governor's "supreme executive power" referenced in *Art. V, Pt. 1, § 1* implies, conceptually, that the Governor has the responsibility to supervise all of the activities of the executive branch. *State v. Simon, 149 Me. 256, 262 (1953); Opinion of Justices, 72 Me. 542 (1881).* But in reality, the "varying degrees of detailed conduct in the executive business of the state" lies with others. *Id.*

2. **Salaries.** The Governor sets salary ranges for certain executive employees. *2 M.R.S. § 6.*

3. **Require Information.** "The Governor may require information from any military officer, or any officer in the executive department, upon any subject relating to the duties of their respective offices." *Art. V, Pt. 1, § 10.* This provision is designed to give the Governor access to information held by executive branch employees that the Governor needs. One interesting question is the degree to which this power may be used to inform the Governor's judgment about

rulemaking employed by agencies under the administrative procedures act. *Compare, Me. Exec. Ord. 12 FY 91/92 with Me. Op. Atty. Gen (Dec. 31, 1991)* (purporting to disapprove of the Order).

4. **Removal.** The power to appoint includes the power to remove. *Longley v. State Employees Appeals Board, 392 A.2d 529 (Me. 1978);* and *Opinion of the Justices, 72 Me. 542, 549-50 (1881).*

   a. **Direct Appointees.** The Governor may remove direct appointees because a Governor is not required to tolerate "weak, incompetent" employees, *id.,* or "work with the appointees of a previous administration, whose loyalties and policies might be wholly different from his own." *Longley v. State Employees Appeals Board, 392 A.2d 529 (Me. 1978).* This is especially so for employees in "policy-making positions" (which are referenced in *5 M.R.S. § 931(1)(K)* and detailed in *5 M.R.S. §§ 932-952*).

   b. **County Sheriffs.** "Whenever the Governor upon complaint, due notice and hearing shall find that a sheriff is not faithfully or efficiently performing any duty imposed upon the sheriff by law, the Governor may remove such sheriff from office and appoint another sheriff to serve for the remainder of the term for which such removed sheriff was elected." *Art. IX, § 10;* and *30-A M.R.S. § 441.*

   c. **Other Civil Officers.** "Every person holding any civil office under this State, may be removed by impeachment, for misdemeanor in office; and every person holding any office, may be removed by the Governor on the address of both branches of the Legislature." *Art. IX, § 5.* It is not clear which specific positions qualify for impeachment. This clause needs to be read together with *Art. IX, § 6* and *5 M.R.S. § 2* cited above, and guidance needs to be taken from pertinent opinions of the Justices and Attorney General. As a starting point, see *Op. Me. Atty. Gen. (Dec. 23, 1982).*

Consider two examples. First, the public advocate who is nominated and confirmed but has no express supervisor. This omission leaves an almost necessary inference that the advocate is supervised by the Governor and thus subject to being cajoled into resignation. But the advocate's statute expressly calls for removal by impeachment. *30-A M.R.S. § 1701(1-A)(E).* And second, the chief medical examiner who is appointed by the Governor and housed with but separated from the Attorney General. *22 M.R.S. § 3022(1).* Again, necessary inference suggests that the Governor technically supervises this position and, because the position is not subject to confirmation, the Governor may possibly also remove the occupant without resorting to impeachment.

5. **Collective Bargaining.** The state Employees Labor Relations Act sets forth the obligations and details of collective bargaining. *26 M.R.S. § 979 et seq.* Management must only bargain those items that are not "prescribed or controlled by public law," *id. at § 979-D (1)(E)(1)*, meaning that the Legislature and Governor can agree to remove items from bargaining and set those terms and conditions by statute.

XIV.
Finance and Budget

A. **Building and Presenting a Biennial Budget.** The process of budgeting is detailed and complex. The primary framework is as follows.

1. The fiscal year of state government starts on July 1st and ends on June 30th each year. *5 M.R.S. § 1501.*

2. By September 1st of even-numbered years, all departments and other entities seeking an appropriation of state funds must submit estimates of their expenditure and appropriation requirements for each fiscal year of the upcoming biennium. *Id. at § 1665(1).*

3. The State Budget Officer uses the revenue projections recommended by the Revenue Forecasting Committee to set the revenue estimate. *Id. at § 1665(3).* The Governor or Governor-elect (hereinafter Governor/elect) then reviews and adjusts the budget requests for the upcoming biennium given this estimate. *Id. at § 1666.*

4. The Bureau of the Budget then prepares a biennial budget that the Governor/elect submits to the Legislature. *Id. at § 1662.*

a. The budget outlines a four-year financial plan for the state government for each fiscal year of the both the upcoming and following biennia. *Id. at § 1664.*

b. More specifically, the budget provides a complete financial plan for each fiscal year of the upcoming biennium. On the revenue side, it sets forth all sources of anticipated revenues and other additional means of financing the expenditures proposed. *Id. at § 1663.* On the expenditures side, the budget sets forth all proposed expenditures for the administration, operation and maintenance of state government; all interest and debt charges; and all expenditures for capital projects. *Id. at § 1663; 5 M.R.S.§ 1581.*

c. The Governor approves and transmits to the Legislature a budget by the Friday following the first Monday in January of the first regular legislative session. A Governor-elect has until early February to so submit. *Id. at § 1666.*

d. The Legislature reviews the submitted budget and by statute is supposed to enact a version 30 days prior to their date of adjournment or, for a Governor-elect, by the first Friday in June. *Id. at § 1666-A.*

B. Budget Must Be Balanced. The constitutional prohibition on pledging more than $2 million of the state's credit without voter approval has been construed to require the state to have a balanced budget. *Art. IX, § 14; Op. Me. Atty. Gen. (Jan. 12, 1990).* The Governor therefore has the duties to:

1. Propose a balanced budget consistent with *5 M.R.S. § 1664(1)(B);*

2. Ensure at signing that an enacted budget is balanced. This is a central purpose of the line-item veto in *Art. IV, Pt. 3, § 2-A*; and

3. Keep a budget balanced during the fiscal year. This is the purpose of the curtailment power delegated by *5 M.R.S. § 1668* and discussed below.

4. Because Maine law expressly requires a biennial budget, and because of the potential consequences following a shorter-term budget, the Attorney General has opined that the Legislature cannot enact a federal-like continuing resolution or other interim short-term budget:

> Maine law requires a biennial budget. Even if it did not do so, any short-term emergency budget, passed with a two-thirds vote, would throw the state into financial uncertainty and would face significant opposition from bondholders, schools, hospitals and thousands of entities to whom the state has continuing and long-term obligations. Compliance with ... consent decree[s] and other court orders would be difficult. Litigation would certainly ensue, and this litigation would be costly and complex. *Op. Me. Atty. Gen. (June 20, 2013).*

C. Supplemental Budget. The Governor may submit during a biennium a budget that supplements or amends the biennial budget initially approved by the Legislature. *Id. at § 1666-A.*

D. Financial Orders. Financial Orders prepared by the Bureau of the Budget and signed by the Governor are the documents by which funds are expended or transferred. *See, for example, id. at §1585* and *§ 1667-B.*

E. **Federal Funds.** The Governor directs the allocation and expenditure of all federal funds and, in doing so, must ensure that federal requirements related to such funds are satisfied. *2 M.R.S. § 4; 5 M.R.S. § 1502.*

F. **Bonds Generally.** A 2/3 vote and popular approval are required for bond issues that "pledge the credit of the state." *Art. IX, § 14.* These are bonds backed by the state's express promise to pay the owed amount. This does not include bonds backed by the real property improved by the bonds such as bonds issued pursuant to *4 M.R.S.A. § 1601 et seq.* Finally, note that proceeds from neither type of bond may be used to fund "current expenditures." *Art. V, Pt. 3, § 5.*

G. **Private Activity Revenue Bonds.** Pursuant to federal law, private activity revenue bond sales by the Finance Authority of Maine and the Maine Health and Higher Educational Facilities Authority are subject to the Governor's approval. *26 U.S.C. § 147(f).*

H. **Contingent Account.** The Governor has an account designated for addressing certain contingencies. *5 M.R.S. § 1507.* The Governor has the discretion to spend limited dollar amounts for projects that fall within certain categories defined by law. *Id.*

I. **Unlawful Expenditures.** The Governor and others authorized to spend appropriated dollars cannot spend money without an appropriation or allocation. *Art. V, Pt. 3, § 4.* The executive must spend within the appropriated categories and amounts. *Lambert v. Ives, CV-91-105 (Me. Super. Ct., May 20, 1991).* It is a class E crime to knowingly spend in excess of an appropriation. *5 M.R.S. § 1583.*

J. Curtailment of Allotments. In order to keep the budget in balance, the Governor has a specific power to spend less than the amounts authorized the Legislature. *5 MRS § 1668.*

1. When the Commissioner of Department of Administrative and Financial Services (DAFS) certifies that authorized expenditures exceed revenues, the Governor may (per the statute but perhaps "shall" given the Constitution's balanced budget requirement) "temporarily curtail allotments equitably," where:

    a. "Temporarily" means that the reduction is not permanent (but see below);

    b. "Curtail" means that an expenditure is reduced and not eliminated; and

    c. "Equitably" means "rationally" but not "evenly" or "fairly." *Id.*; *Butterfield v. McKernan, CV-91-29 (Me. Super. Ct., Jan. 17, 1991); Ops. Me. Atty. Gen. No. 90-1, 91-14, 95-7, 02-2.*

2. The Governor can only curtail:

    a. up to the amount necessary to ensure "that expenditures will not exceed anticipated revenues," *5 MRS § 1668;* and

    b. "insofar as practicable ... consistent with the intent of the Legislature in authorizing [the] expenditures." *Id.*

3. Once the Governor acts, the Legislature may enact a revised budget (one that perhaps the Governor proposes to align with the curtailment order) that does permanently change the underlying appropriations. Such an amended budget would supersede the Governor's curtailment order. But if the Legislature fails to enact an amended budget or

fails to override a veto of an amended budget, the Governor's action stands.

4. Because the Legislature is thc source in delegating the curtailment power to the executive, and because the Legislature retains the opportunity to displace the Governor's executive order through its enactment and override powers, the curtailment statute does not usurp the Legislature's appropriations power in violation of separation of powers. *Butterfield v. McKernan, CV-91-29 (Me. Super. Ct., Jan. 17, 1991); 82 Yale L. J. 1636 (1973).*

5. The separation of powers clause in Article III effectively limits the Governor's authority to order curtailment of Judicial Branch expenditures. However, as a matter of practice in the 1991 financial crisis, and at other times, the Judicial Branch upon the Governor's request, engaged in a voluntary curtailment of its expenditures.

6. For a reliable template of an executive order curtailing allotments, *see Me. Exec. Ord. 11 FY 90/91.*

K. Budgetary Shutdown of State Government

1. The biennial budget is state government's authority to incur the cost of and pay for its services. *5 M.R.S. § 1663.* Maine law requires that a biennial budget be enacted and in effect by July 1st of the first year of the biennium. *Id. at § 1501.* If such a budget is not timely enacted, there is a void in the state's authority to incur and pay for such costs and therefore provide services. *Accord, 43 Op. U.S. Atty. Gen. 24 (1980).*

2. The effect of state government failing to provide essential services presents an "occurrence or imminent threat of widespread or severe damage, injury or loss of life or property resulting from ... any ... man-made cause," *37-B*

M.R.S. § 703 (2), and therefore an emergency within the meaning of *id. at § 701 et seq.*

3. To ensure essential governmental services are provided, the Governor may proclaim an emergency under *id. at § 742(1)(A),* trigger the authorities under *id. at § 741* and *§ 742,* and use executive and financial orders to provide essential services. *Me. Exec. Ords. 1-7 FY 91/92.*

4. "Essential services" have been defined as those duties and functions that "minimize the risk of direct and imminent injury to persons, or minimize the risk of direct, imminent and substantial harm to property, or that serve to repair any such injury to persons or harm to property or are essential to completing that portion of the law-making process that will relieve the state of emergency, or … are necessary or appropriate to meet additional needs." *Me. Exec. Ord. 1 FY 91/92.* Essential services also include, by force of the supremacy (*U.S. Const. Art. VI, ¶ 2)* and spending (*id. at Art. I, § 8, cl. 1),* clauses of the federal Constitution, those services required to comply with federal law.

5. The Governor may govern under this rubric until a biennial budget is enacted, if at all, into law.

XV.
Administering Elections

A. **Introduction.** Governors have numerous specific and detailed election-related duties under Title 21-A in certifying and proclaiming certain elections and the results thereof. The following are leading examples.

B. **Certifications.** The Governor:

1. Issues election certificates, *21-A M.R.S. § 724;*
2. Certifies Maine's presidential electors, *id. at § 803*; and
3. Issues election certificates to duly elected registers of deeds, *33 M.R.S. § 602.*

C. **Proclamations.** The Governor issues proclamations when there is a:

1. Referenda and initiatives, *Art. IV, Pt. 3, §§ 17-19;*
2. Maine Senate seat vacancy, *Art. IV, Pt. 2, § 5* and *21-A M.R.S. § 381*;
3. Maine House vacancy, *id.at § 382*;
4. Congressional vacancy, *id. at § 392*;

5. Special election, *id. at. § 366*; and

6. Election tie, *id. at § 732.*

D. Other. The Governor:

1. Receives tabulations used in recounts, *id. at. § 737-A;* and

2. Issues summons to elected representatives (*Art. IV, Pt. 1, § 5)* and senators (*Art. IV, Pt. 2, § 4)* to attend a new Legislature.

XVI.
Other

A. Relations with the Secretary of State. The Secretary of State is required to "attend" the Governor. *Art. V, Pt. 2, § 3.* This is an awkwardly phrased provision of the constitution, but it appears to mean that the Governor may require the secretary to participate or otherwise assist in matters related to the Governor's responsibilities.

B. Relations with Native American Tribes. Numerous state and federal laws define the relationship between Maine and its Native Americans. The fundamental state law is the Act to Implement the Maine Indian Claims Settlement. *30 M.R.S. § 6201 et seq.*

C. Relations with the United States

1. Military Base Realignment and Closure

a. The Base Realignment and Closure (BRAC) process is the congressionally authorized process for the Department of Defense (DoD) to reorganize its base structure to better support forces, increase operational readiness, and facilitate new practices. *10 U.S.C. § 2687.*

b. BRAC rounds come approximately every 10 years but there has not been a BRAC round since 2005. There were five BRAC rounds between 1988 and 2005. In the 1991 round, Maine lost Loring Air Force Base. In the 2005 round, Maine lost Brunswick Naval Air Station but saved Portsmouth Naval Shipyard.

c. In the event of a BRAC round, the economic impacts to the state can be in the billions of dollars. The Governor therefore works very closely with the Congressional Delegation during the months-long process.

d. For an account of how BRAC works in general and how it worked specifically in 2005, see *Langhauser, 2005 BRAC Process: The Case to Save Maine's Bases, Me. Pol. Rev. 14.1 (2005) at https://digitalcommons.library.umaine.edu/mpr/vol14/iss1/9.*

2. **Eminent Domain Transfers to the United States.** The Governor is authorized to take certain lands and provide for certain transfers to the United States. *1 M.R.S. §§ 12-14.*

D. Relations with Canada. The Governor appoints the Maine-Canada Trade Ombudsman whose office advises the Governor and coordinates state policy and state actions on commerce and other relations with individuals, businesses, and governmental entities in Canada. *5 M.R.S. § 261 et seq.*

Appendix

Federal Court Transcript of Ruling for Governor's Intervention to Defend in Opposition to the Attorney General the Constitutionality of a State Statute

Gallagher v. Diamond

United States District Court for the District of Maine
October 26, 1990, Decided
CIVIL NO. 90-0256-B

(Impertinent portions omitted.)

Reporter

1990 U.S. Dist. LEXIS 20931 *

J. PATRICK GALLAGHER, et als., Plaintiffs v. G. WILLIAM DIAMOND, Defendant

Judges: Judge D. BROCK HORNBY.

Opinion by: D. BROCK HORNBY

FINDINGS OF FACT AND CONCLUSIONS OF LAW

Pursuant to notice, the above-entitled matter came on for hearing before Hon. D. Brock Hornby, Judge, United States District Court, District of Maine, at the United States Courthouse, Bangor, Maine, on October 26, 1990, at which time and place the following proceedings were had:

FINDINGS OF FACT AND CONCLUSIONS OF LAW

(In open court at 8:30 a.m. on October 26, 1990.)

THE COURT: Good morning counsel.

(Replies of "Good morning.")

THE COURT: I appreciate your coming back this morning. I regret that I was not able to give you a decision last night, but we were here, I think, until well after 6 on the other matter, in any event. I didn't think it was appropriate **[*2]** to keep the lawyers and parties in that matter waiting longer.

I'm going to ask your indulgence as I give my decision, because I have a lot of notes from yesterday afternoon and evening. So I may be paper-shuffling at times. So just bear with me as I do that.

First of all, I want to again compliment all of you on your presentation of the merits in this matter. These are not simple issues. They're difficult issues. And I think that your presentations were excellent and in accordance with the standards of what I would expect from members of the bar of this court. I just wanted to mention that again. I thought you did do a very good job.

I do remain troubled by the procedural posture of the case, with the Attorney General for the Secretary of the State saying that the statute is unconstitutional, but that a legitimate argument can be made the other way, and we'll let the Governor make it. That raises in federal court, as you know, concerns for case for controversy. Usually two parties can simply resolve the dispute and take care of it, and then there's no jurisdiction by the federal court. But here I have, in addition, the Governor's motion to intervene and this whole line-up of the **[*3]** parties is very troubling to me sitting as a federal judge dealing with these matters.

On August the 2nd, as you well know, the Opinion of the Justices stated, and I will quote two paragraphs:

> "The statutes simply do not provide a way for placing a nominee on the ballot for the general election when no candidate for nomination obtains the required minimum number of 25 votes in the primary. In such circumstances, a write-in candidacy remains the available alternative for the general election.
>
> "We are mindful that restrictions on access to the ballot present concerns of constitutional dimension. We are persuaded, however, that the State of Maine may legally require that all candidates for nomination make a preliminary showing of substantial support. The requirement that a nominee receive 25 votes is an even-handed restriction applicable to all and is reasonably designed to protect the integrity of the electoral process."

And the justices went on to cite the U.S. Supreme Court decisions of *Jeness v. Fortson and Anderson v. Celebrezze.*

I, frankly, find it astonishing that the Secretary of State, an official of the State of Maine, finds it appropriate, in face of the justices' [*4] explicit language rendered so recently on both Maine law and on the statute's constitutionality, that he considers it appropriate to waive any defense when the state statute's constitutionality is challenged in federal court.

Now, to be sure, the Opinion of the Justices is an advisory ruling, but it is obtained and issued for a purpose, and it surely deserves credence by all state authorities, at least until they have litigated the matter to a final decision in a state or federal court. It may be that the Attorney General believes that his office cannot defend the constitutionality of the statute because of earlier expressed misgivings in briefing the statutory interpretation issue in connection with the justices' advisory ruling.

I have some doubts even about that position, since it seems proper that, once having received the ruling, whatever his previous doubts, the Attorney General, the chief law enforcement officer of the state, should defend the ruling. I can't imagine that every time that the Attorney General's office loses a case, that it's disqualified on all future issues that involve the same law.

But, nevertheless, if it was professionally impossible to defend the statute [*5] because of the previous position taken by the Attorney General, an available alternative was simply to authorize the Secretary of State to hire other lawyers who could defend the statute in accordance with the Opinion of the Justices.

That has not been done. Instead, this federal court is faced with a challenge to a state statute that governs what names appear on the ballot, where both the Secretary of State, who is responsible for printing ballots, and the Attorney General, the state's chief law enforcement officer, concede its unconstitutionality as applied, even on the face of the very recent and contrary opinion of the justices. And then the Governor, from whom the plaintiffs no longer seek relief and who is, therefore, no longer a party to the action, has now moved to intervene to defend the constitutionality of the statute. The Governor seeks standing to intervene by virtue of his constitutional obligation under the Maine Constitution, Article V, Part 1, Section 12, to "take care that the laws be faithfully executed."

I have some doubt whether that constitutional provision entitles the Governor to interfere in the statutory duties of other state officials; and I refer to the [*6] opinion of the justices at *147 Me. 410, 105 A.2d 454 (1952).*

The sole issue at stake in this litigation is the obligation of the Secretary of State in preparing ballots; specifically, whether he shall list Democratic candidates in House Districts 143 and 145, or leave them off the ballots, so that only write-in votes are possible for the Democratic candidates. I note that the equivalent concern for a Republican candidate in House District 150 that was originally raised is no longer pressed by the plaintiffs.

The plaintiffs object to the Governor's motion to intervene, contending that the Governor has no standing and that only the Secretary of State is a proper party, since no relief is being sought against the Governor, and nothing that takes place here will affect what he does.

Now, the question of intervention in federal court is ordinarily governed by Rule 24. Rule 24(a)(2) provides for intervention as of right, and it requires that the Governor claim, and I quote, "an interest relating to the property or transaction which is the subject of the action."

There's no property here. The transaction, if there is one, is to place particular candidates' names on a ballot. [*7] The Governor has no role in that process.

Permissive intervention is governed by Rule 24(b)(2), as interpreted by the First Circuit Court of Appeals in *International Paper Company v. Jay, 887 F.2d 338*, a First Circuit, 1989 decision. It requires that the Governor demonstrate, among other things, "a direct and substantial interest in the subject matter of the litigation."

Well, the subject matter of this litigation is whose names will appear on the ballot in House Districts 143 and 145. The Governor's office has no direct and substantial interest in that question. It is the Secretary of State's duty to administer elections and print ballots under the Maine Election Law statutes in Title 21-A, for example, Sections 21 and Section 376.

If the Governor's duty to take care that the laws be faithfully executed were sufficient, the Governor would be entitled to intervene in every lawsuit where he disagreed with the position taken by the Attorney General. I do not believe that principle could be limited to election law cases or cases where there is a recent advisory opinion of the justices, or suchlike.

On the other hand, the Attorney General's office, representing the **[*8]** Secretary of State, does not object to the motion for permissive intervention. The Attorney General's position here is confusing to the court, for the Attorney General continues to reiterate that the Attorney General is solely responsible for representing state officials in litigation. The Attorney General goes onto say, however, that his office has authorized the Governor to obtain private lawyers to represent the Governor in this matter. But that was apparently at a time when the Governor was a named defendant and the plaintiffs were seeking to have the Governor take specific action.

The fact that the Attorney General's office believes that it cannot represent the Governor because of its previous position does not address the question whether the Governor's office has any standing to intervene in the matter as it is now framed.

If the Attorney General, representing the Secretary of State, believes, as it says, that the Governor has a legitimate position—in other words, that the legislation may be constitutional—that would seem to be ground for having the Secretary of State defend this action, in light of the advisory opinion of the justices, and authorize the Secretary of **[*9]** State to engage private lawyers. . . .

So I remain uncertain and as to what it is that the Attorney General's Office believes it's agreeing to in acceding to the motion to intervene. If the Secretary of State had deferred to the opinion of the justices, defended the constitutionality of the statute, and retained a private law firm to do so if the Attorney General could not represent him, this whole matter would be much more straightforward.

Nevertheless, I have to deal with what is presented to me, and it is clear from United States Supreme Court case law and the treatises that when a federal court is confronted with a situation where a governmental agency concedes the unconstitutionality of a statute in response to a plaintiff's complaint, a Legislature can be allowed to intervene to defend the validity of the statute, for example, the case of *Immigration and Naturalization Service v. Chadha, 462 U.S. 919, 77 L. Ed. 2d 317, 103 S. Ct. 2764.*

The Governor, who in most instances signs legislation in order for it to become effective and who alternatively has veto power over legislation, surely has a comparable interest in the constitutionality of legislation. [***10**] So, under the *Chadha* reasoning, he should, therefore, likewise be permitted to defend such legislation in federal court when an executive official refuses to.

Therefore, I conclude that under reasoning like that of the Supreme Court in *Chadha*, its language there, that independent of the language of Rule 24, a motion to intervene should be allowed; and, that if it is allowed, a case for controversy thereby exists. The Attorney General's Office, moreover, has stated that if a decree is not entered by this court, the Secretary of State will not actually print the names of the two Democrats seeking to be on the ballot.

And so I conclude again, under the *Chadha* rationale, that for that reason as well, there is a real case for controversy for me to decide. And so, despite the tangled web of who is taking what position, I ultimately conclude that the motion to intervene should be granted at least insofar as to permit the Governor to defend the constitutionality of the statute. I do this, as I say, with some doubts as to his role given the 1952 opinion of the justices and the requirements of Rule 24. But since the Attorney General appears not to object, and since *Chadha* counsels [***11**] that other agencies of government with an interest in the constitutionality of the statute should be permitted to defend it, I will allow the intervention and entertain the Governor's argument.

I understand that the plaintiffs would prefer to have to deal only with the Secretary of State and the Attorney General, but since the plaintiffs are asking this federal court to be part of declaring a state statute unconstitutional, I have concluded that the plaintiffs must put up with someone defending the statute.

I therefore address the merits……

[***22**] I conclude that the state's interest in the integrity of the primary election process and in insuring that major party candidates who appear on the general election ballot have some minimum level of support reflected by secret ballot choices made in the polling booth at a primary election, and in insuring some minimum level of voter awareness, is a compelling state interest.

[***24**] I conclude, therefore, that the statutory measure is narrowly tailored to serve the compelling state interest.

[***25**] I conclude that the statute must be upheld against the constitutional attack … Accordingly, the clerk shall enter judgment upholding the constitutionality of the statute against the plaintiff's attack.

Made in the USA
Monee, IL
04 November 2026

67387554R00085